Language Teacher Education for a Global Society

"There is no other book like this for preparing more effective L2 teachers. All classroom teachers will benefit from reading it and giving careful consideration as to how their own practice in the classroom can be improved."

Neil Anderson, Brigham Young University, USA

"Offering a wide-ranging and high quality conceptualization, the coverage is masterly, employing the profound reach of scholarship that the author has demonstrated in previous publications. This book could be a core reference in the field for years to come, one to which other attempts would be compared, and one on which other writers with more specific interests would draw."

Julian Edge, University of Manchester, UK

The field of second/foreign language teacher education is calling out for a coherent and comprehensive framework for teacher preparation in these times of accelerating economic, cultural, and educational globalization. Responding to this call, this book introduces a state-of-the-art model for developing prospective and practicing teachers into strategic thinkers, exploratory researchers, and transformative teachers. The model includes five modules: Knowing, Analyzing, Recognizing, Doing, and Seeing (KARDS). Its goal is to help teachers understand

- How to build a viable professional, personal and procedural knowledge-base;
- How to analyze learner needs, motivation and autonomy;
- How to recognize their own identities, beliefs and values;
- How to do teaching, theorizing and dialogizing; and
- How to see their own teaching acts from learner, teacher, and observer perspectives.

Providing a scaffold for teachers to build a holistic understanding of what happens in the language classroom, this model eventually enables them to theorize what they practice and practice what they theorize. With its strong scholarly foundation and its supporting reflective tasks and exploratory projects, this book is immensely useful for students, practicing teachers, teacher educators, and educational researchers who are interested in exploring the complexity of language teacher education.

B. Kumaravadivelu is Professor, Department of Linguistics and Language Development, San Jose State University.

ESL & Applied Linguistics Professional Series
Eli Hinkel, Series Editor

Kumaravadivelu • *Language Teacher Education for a Global Society: A Modular Model for Knowing, Analyzing, Recognizing, Doing, and Seeing*

Vandergrift/Goh • *Teaching and Learning Second Language Listening: Metacognition in Action*

LoCastro • *Pragmatics for Language Educators: A Sociolinguistics Perspective*

Nelson • *Intelligibility in World Englishes: Theory and Practice*

Nation/Macalister, Eds. • *Case Studies in Language Curriculum Design*

Johnson/Golumbek, Eds. • *Research on Second Language Teacher Education: A Sociocultural Perspective on Professional Development*

Hinkel, Ed. • *Handbook of Research in Second Language Teaching and Learning Volume II*

Nassaji/Fotos • *Teaching Grammar in Second Language Classrooms: Integrating Form-Focused Instruction in Communicative Context*

Murray/Christison • *What English Language Teachers Need to Know Volume I: Understanding Learning*

Murray/Christison • *What English Language Teachers Need to Know Volume II: Facilitating Learning*

Wong/Waring • *Conversation Analysis and Second Language Pedagogy: A Guide for ESL/EFL Teachers*

Nunan/Choi, Eds. • *Language and Culture: Reflective Narratives and the Emergence of Identity*

Braine • *Nonnative Speaker English Teachers: Research, Pedagogy, and Professional Growth*

Burns • *Doing Action Research in English Language Teaching: A Guide for Practitioners*

Nation/Macalister • *Language Curriculum Design*

Birch • *The English Language Teacher and Global Civil Society*

Johnson • *Second Language Teacher Education: A Sociocultural Perspective*

Nation • *Teaching ESL/EFL Reading and Writing*

Nation/Newton • *Teaching ESL/EFL Listening and Speaking*

Kachru/Smith • *Cultures, Contexts, and World Englishes*

McKay/Bokhosrt-Heng • *International English in its Sociolinguistic Contexts: Towards a Socially Sensitive EIL Pedagogy*

Christison/Murray, Eds. • *Leadership in English Language Education: Theoretical Foundations and Practical Skills for Changing Times*

McCafferty/Stam, Eds. • *Gesture: Second Language Acquisition and Classroom Research*

Liu • *Idioms: Description, Comprehension, Acquisition, and Pedagogy*

Chapelle/Enright/Jamison, Eds. • *Building a Validity Argument for the Test of English as a Foreign Language*™

Kondo-Brown/Brown, Eds. • *Teaching Chinese, Japanese, and Korean Heritage Students: Curriculum Needs, Materials, and Assessments*

Youmans • *Chicano-Anglo Conversations: Truth, Honesty, and Politeness*

Birch • *English L2 Reading: Getting to the Bottom, Second Edition*

Luk/Lin • *Classroom Interactions as Cross-cultural Encounters: Native Speakers in EFL Lessons*

Levy/Stockwell • *CALL Dimensions: Issues and Options in Computer Assisted Language Learning*

Nero, Ed. • *Dialects, Englishes, Creoles, and Education*

Basturkmen • *Ideas and Options in English for Specific Purposes*

Kumaravadivelu • *Understanding Language Teaching: From Method to Postmethod*

McKay • *Researching Second Language Classrooms*

Egbert/Petrie, Eds. • *CALL Research Perspectives*

Canagarajah, Ed. • *Reclaiming the Local in Language Policy and Practice*

Adamson • *Language Minority Students in American Schools: An Education in English*

Fotos/Browne, Eds. • *New Perspectives on CALL for Second Language Classrooms*

Hinkel • *Teaching Academic ESL Writing: Practical Techniques in Vocabulary and Grammar*

Hinkel/Fotos, Eds. • *New Perspectives on Grammar Teaching in Second Language Classrooms*

Hinkel • *Second Language Writers' Text: Linguistic and Rhetorical Features*

Visit **www.routledge.com/education** for additional information on titles in the ESL & Applied Linguistics Professional Series

Language Teacher Education For A Global Society

A Modular Model for Knowing, Analyzing, Recognizing, Doing, and Seeing

B. Kumaravadivelu

Routledge
Taylor & Francis Group

NEW YORK AND LONDON

First published 2012
by Routledge
711 Third Avenue, New York, NY 10017

Simultaneously published in the UK
by Routledge
2 Park Square, Milton Park, Abingdon, Oxon OX14 4RN

Routledge is an imprint of the Taylor & Francis Group, an informa business

Library of Congress Cataloging in Publication Data
Kumaravadivelu, B., 1948-
Language teacher education for a global society : a modular model for knowing,
analyzing, recognizing, doing, and seeing / B. Kumaravadivelu. -- 1st ed.
p. cm. -- (ESL & applied linguistics professional series)
Includes bibliographical references and index.
1. Language teachers--Training of. I. Title.
P53.85.K86 2011
418.0071--dc23
2011029808

ISBN13: 978-0-415-87737-4 (hbk)
ISBN13: 978-0-415-87738-1 (pbk)
ISBN13: 978-0-203-83253-0 (ebk)

Typeset in Bembo
by Taylor & Francis Books

Printed and bound in the United States of America on acid-free paper by
Walsworth Publishing Company, Marceline, MO

SUSTAINABLE
FORESTRY
INITIATIVE

Certified Sourcing
www.sfiprogram.org
SFI-00555
The SFI label applies to the text stock.

Dedicated to
those who teach and delight

தாம்இன் புறுவது உலகுஇன் புறக்கண்டு

காமுறுவர் கற்றறிந் தார்

The learned long for more learning not only because it delights them but also because they can delight the world with their learning.

(*Thirukural,* verse 399, circa 100 A.D.)

CONTENTS

PREFACE

This book has been a long time coming. Eleven years, to be exact. I made the first formal presentation on the proposed modular model for language teacher education in March 2000, at the 34th Annual TESOL Convention held in Vancouver, Canada. I am writing this Preface immediately after I returned from the University of Aston, Birmingham, England where, in July 2011, I gave a plenary talk at the 7th BAAL (British Association for Applied Linguistics) Special Interest Group on Language Learning and Teaching—my last presentation on the model before I finally managed to place the manuscript in the hands of the publishers.

In between Vancouver and Birmingham, I have given plenary talks, keynote addresses or guest lectures on the model at the 4th International Conference on Language Teacher Education, University of Minnesota, USA (June, 2005), at Hong Kong Baptist University, Hong Kong (April, 2008), at Hong Kong Institute of Education, Hong Kong (May, 2008), at the ESEA Conference in Singapore (December, 2008), at the 2nd biennial International Conference of the Australian Council of TESOL Associations, Gold Coast, Australia (July, 2010), at the 3rd International Seminar on Professional Development in Foreign Language Education in Medillin, Colombia (August, 2010), and at the Defense Language Institute, Monterrey, California (February, 2011). This book is indeed the fruit of several years of reflection, review, and renewal.

While my thoughts on the model have evolved considerably over the years, what has remained constant, as the title of my March 2000 TESOL presentation— "KARDS for teacher education"—shows, is the acronym KARDS, standing for Knowing, Analyzing, Recognizing, Doing, and Seeing. The choice of dynamic verbs, rather than static nouns, to refer to the componential parts of the model is deliberate. So is the choice of the *modular* makeup of the model. My intention has always been to move away from traditional ways of designing linear, product-based, transmission-oriented, discrete courses, and towards new ways of designing cyclical, process-based, transformation-oriented, holistic modules.

The driving force behind these choices is the realization that merely tinkering with the existing system of language teacher education will not suffice to meet the challenges posed by accelerating economic, cultural, and educational globalization, and that what is surely and sorely needed is no less than a radical restructuring of language teacher education. This contention is premised upon five interconnected propositions that are as simple as they are straightforward: (a) any meaningful, context-sensitive pedagogic knowledge can emerge only from the classroom; (b) it is the practicing teacher who is well placed to produce and apply that knowledge; (c) current approaches to language teacher education are mostly aimed at preparing teachers to become consumers, not producers, of pedagogic knowledge; (d) the fast evolving global society with its incessant and increased flow of peoples, goods and ideas across the world is placing huge responsibilities on the shoulders of student teachers, practicing teachers and teacher educators; and therefore (e) we need to re-view and re-vision language teacher education if we are serious about helping language teaching professionals become strategic thinkers, exploratory researchers and transformative intellectuals.

Outline

The book is written in seven chapters. In the introductory chapter, I recall the tremendous strides that have been made in the last few years to advance the frontiers of knowledge in the field of TESOL language teacher education. However, an accumulation of insights in a disjointed fashion can only lead to a limited and limiting understanding. Therefore, I stress the need to pull together various strands of thought in order to design a cogent and comprehensive model for language teacher education. Accordingly, I present the rationale for and the essentials of such a model in terms of five global perspectives (postnational, postmodern, postcolonial, post-transmission, and postmethod), and three operating principles (particularity, practicality, and possibility). I contend that these fundamental perspectives and principles provide the conceptual underpinnings necessary for designing a model for language teacher education that is sensitive to global and local exigencies.

The next five chapters deal with each of the five componential modules: Knowing, Analyzing, Recognizing, Doing, and Seeing. In the chapter on Knowing, I express my skepticism about the pedagogic value of the bewildering array of labels and definitions for teacher knowledge one finds in the literature. Instead, I opt for a simpler frame of reference: professional knowledge, procedural knowledge, and personal knowledge. The first pertains to the intellectual content of a discipline produced and disseminated by experts, the second to the instructional management strategies needed to create and sustain a classroom environment in which the desired learning outcome is made possible, and the third to the individual teacher's sense of plausibility, a sense of what works and what doesn't. I stress the importance of helping teachers develop their personal knowledge.

The focus of the next chapter is on learner needs, motivation and autonomy. I point out how learner needs are shifting towards the development of genuine communicative abilities required to exploit the unlimited possibilities that the globalized job market has opened up. Also shifting are motivational factors that now render the traditional concept of integrative motivation inadequate because of the on-going cultural globalization and its impact on individual and national identities, and because of the Internetization of information systems. I note how researchers in the field of L2 motivation research are now turning to recent developments in cognitive psychology, to postmodern thoughts, and to critical pedagogy, and explain how these developments might shape teaching and teacher education.

Clearly, teachers' developing knowledge systems, and their awareness of learner needs, motivation, and autonomy can be effectively used only if they recognize the teaching Self that they bring with them to the practice of everyday teaching. In Chapter 4, therefore, I turn to the importance of recognizing teacher identities, beliefs, and values. I put these personal attributes in a broader philosophical, psychological, and sociological landscape by outlining the concepts of identity and identity formation, beliefs and belief systems, and values and value judgments. I then connect these general concepts to specific pedagogic imperatives drawing insights from general education as well as from the field of English language teaching. I also show how teachers can learn to interrogate their teaching Self using critical auto-ethnography as an investigative tool, and to draw a self-portrait connecting the personal, the professional, the pedagogical, and the political.

In the next chapter, I focus on how the doing of teaching, theorizing, and dialogizing are all closely intertwined, and that they nurture each other in a cycle of formation and transformation. Teaching is presented as a reflective activity which at once shapes and is shaped by the doing of theorizing which in turn is bolstered by the collaborative process of dialogic inquiry. The doing of teaching is marked by efforts to maximize learning opportunities and to mentor personal transformation. I explain how the construction of even a personal theory of practice has to be carried out collaboratively and dialogically. I also highlight the types of teacher research that can potentially help teachers theorize from the classroom.

An important prerequisite for meaningful teacher research to take place is the ability of teachers to *see* what happens in the classroom. Arguing that *seeing* has seldom received the kind of attention it really deserves and demands, I begin the chapter on seeing with a philosophical rendering of the concept, and go on to discuss three different forms of seeing: *seeing-in, seeing-as*, and *seeing-that*. I show that *seeing-that* is a higher form of seeing, one that is critically mediated by seeing and knowing, helping us forge new connections between our conceptual knowledge and perceptual knowledge. I then emphasize the importance of seeing the learner, teacher, and observer perspectives to derive useable insights about language lessons. I also present methodological procedures and illustrative examples that show how the *seeing-that* form of observation is capable of assisting participants to make the connection between seeing and knowing.

I try to put all these together in the concluding chapter. Highlighting the salient features of the modular model, I reflect on the prospects and problems of designing a context-sensitive model for language teacher education. I start with a brief note on the nature of models and modules and then consider possible ways of designing and delivering a model that is sensitive to local demands and responsive to global forces. I also discuss the challenge of change facing any innovative educational endeavor. I show how local practitioners can use the essentials of the model as broad guidelines to conceive and construct what they consider to be a locally relevant language teacher education program.

Readership

Given its scope, style and substance, the book is geared towards the needs of many players in the field of language teacher education. It is intended for student teachers who are being introduced to the field of language education, for practicing teachers who wish to enhance their knowledge and skill about teaching, for teacher educators who are looking for a cogent volume that can be used in pre-service as well as in-service programs, and for educational researchers who are interested in exploring the complexity of language teacher education. It is also intended to provide a necessary conceptual framework and practical strategies for those who might wish to design context-specific models of language teacher education. With its global focus that is sensitive to local exigencies, the book is aimed at a wide variety of national and international audiences. Although most of the illustrative examples are drawn from the field of *English* language teaching and teacher education, the book is written for those who are interested in language teaching and teacher education in general.

All the chapters except the last one end with (a) Rapid Reader Response; (b) Reflective Tasks; and (c) Exploratory Projects. The idea of Rapid Reader Response is adapted from the *One-Minute Feedback* strategy pioneered at Harvard School of Education. I have modified it to have a cluster of four textual questions that attempt to elicit a quick, stream of consciousness response from readers about the chapter that they have just finished reading. Therefore, the same four questions are repeated in all the six chapters. Unlike Rapid Reader Response, Reflective Tasks are designed to prompt extended and in-depth responses for specific questions that require critical reflection on the part of the reader. Exploratory Projects are meant to give opportunities for prospective and present teachers to conduct their own situated investigations aimed at relating the issues raised in a particular chapter to their specific learning and teaching context. I hope that these activities will facilitate the reader's deeper engagement with the text and the context thereby promoting a better understanding of the issues involved.

In writing this book, my aims have been, first, to present some of the latest scholarship about language teaching and teacher education in a coordinated and accessible way; second, to highlight the challenges as well as opportunities facing the field of language teacher education in a global society that is impacted by the processes of economic, cultural and educational globalization; and third, to explore the essentials of a cogent and comprehensive model that has the potential to fundamentally transform the way we conceive and conduct language teacher preparation. This has been a long and complex pursuit.

ACKNOWLEDGMENTS

I have been greatly helped in this pursuit by a host of people who traversed my personal and professional life. First and foremost, I wish to thank all those (too many to name) who attended my talks delivered in five different countries, endured my still-evolving thoughts, and offered critical comments which have certainly enhanced the quality of my work. I am grateful to Naomi Silverman for her unending stream of professional care and personal kindness, and to Eli Hinkel for her unfailing faith in my abilities. Thanks also go to my external reviewers Professor Neil Anderson, Brigham Young University, USA, and Professor Julian Edge, University of Manchester, UK for their critical comments and helpful suggestions. I am thankful to Jean Shiota, Faculty Lab Coordinator at the office of Academic Technology, who was always ready and willing to help me with computer graphics.

On the home front, I am indebted to my wife Revathi who has always been a source of solid support and a steady supply of green tea. She took upon herself extraordinary domestic responsibilities (in spite of her own professorial demands) especially in the last two months of my writing so that I could finish the project without asking for yet another extension of the deadline. My children Anand and Chandrika offered me more than their usual diversion this time. Anand pitched in to type the classroom transcripts I have used in this book, thereby saving me valuable time. His only comment was that I use the term *pedagogy* too much. Chandrika glanced through my last chapter and said, "it's too cheesy." Clearly, I still have much to learn.

1

(RE)VISIONING LANGUAGE TEACHER EDUCATION

> A cartload of bricks is not a house;
> we want a principle, a system, an integration.
> (Michel Serres 2004: 2)

1.0 Introduction

Teacher education is not just about teachers and their education. It is infinitely more than the two put together. It is often called upon to tackle critical issues and questions that go far beyond their boundaries. In a comprehensive and authoritative report titled *Studying Teacher Education*, two leading American educationists, Marilyn Cochran-Smith and Kenneth Zeichner (2005: 2–3) make it abundantly clear that education and teacher education are social institutions that pose moral, ethical, social, philosophical, and ideological questions.

They caution that

> there are not likely to be good answers to the most important questions about teacher preparation unless they are driven by sophisticated theoretical frameworks about the nature of good teaching and the nature of teachers' learning.
>
> *(ibid.: 3–4)*

According to them, any sophisticated theoretical framework must necessarily take into account not only issues such as teachers' knowledge, skills, dispositions, cognition, and beliefs but also factors such as educational, social, cultural, and ideological movements as well as major swings in the political pendulum. To this long list, we now have to add global economic trends and global cultural flows.

If there is a need for a comprehensive framework for teacher preparation in the field of general education, which has witnessed substantial exploration and expansion in the last fifty years, then, clearly, the need for such a framework in the relatively nascent field of second and foreign language (L2) teacher education is even greater. Following the lead given by general educationists, applied linguists have explored several aspects of L2 teacher education. Just in the last fifteen years, we have witnessed an impressive array of valuable work on topics as varied as teacher cognition (Woods 1996, Borg 2006), teacher research (Freeman 1998), teacher freedom (Brumfit 2001), teacher self-development (Edge 2002), teacher narrative (Johnson & Golombek 2002), teacher coherence (Clarke 2003), teacher values (Johnston 2003), teacher expertise (Tsui 2003), teacher experience (Senior 2006), teacher philosophy (Crookes 2009), and teacher reflection (Edge 2011). These investigations and interpretations have undoubtedly expanded our knowledge base. However, accumulation of insights in a disjointed fashion can only lead to a limited and limiting understanding. What is sorely missing in our field, as in general education, is a cogent, coherent and comprehensive model that pulls together various strands of thought in order to help student teachers, teachers, teacher educators and researchers see "the pattern that connects."

What might constitute the foundational stones needed for constructing a comprehensive model for L2 teacher education? I discuss them under two broad categories: globalizing perspectives, and operating principles.

1.1 Globalizing Perspectives

In a concerted effort to respond to the impact of globalization on education and teacher education, ten leading institutions from ten different countries including Australia, China, Denmark, Singapore, the UK, and the USA have formed what is called "The International Alliance of Leading Education Institutes." Founded at a meeting in Singapore in 2007, the Alliance acts as a think-tank aimed at generating ideas and identifying trends to serve as a collective voice on important educational issues. Appropriately, it took up the challenging issue of teacher education as its primary task. In its first report titled *Transforming Teacher Education,* the Alliance concludes (2008: 14):

> Notwithstanding their origins, commonalities and differences, all systems of teacher preparation have to rethink their core assumptions and processes in the new global context.

What exactly is the new global context that confronts teacher education today? It seems to me that there are at least five inter-connected perspectives that can help us understand the fast-evolving global context. They are: postnational, postmodern, postcolonial, post-transmission, and postmethod perspectives. The first three are related to broader historical, political, and sociocultural developments across the world while the last two pertain more narrowly to language teacher education.

I frame these global perspectives in terms of "posts" because we all live in a world of "posts." The epistemology of the "post" has facilitated substantial knowledge production in the humanities and social sciences, and it offers a useful site to anchor one's thoughts on broader forces that impact on education and teacher education. A common understanding of the term "post" is that it connotes something that comes "afterwards" in time. In the specialized field of cultural studies, however, it does not merely connote a progression in time, but rather a fundamental shift from one conceptual understanding to another, thereby marking a sustainable challenge to existing paradigms of knowledge. Consequently, the "post" produces a heightened awareness of historical, political, and cultural movements that shape and reshape human beliefs and behaviors. Thus, chronologically speaking, postmodernism comes after modernism. But, it stands for a more radical conceptualization and interpretation of the human condition than the one offered by modernism, as explained below. Clearly, the shift is more than temporal. Keeping such an understanding of "posts" in mind, let us briefly consider the five globalizing perspectives.

1.1.1 The Postnational Perspective

The idea of a nation-state emerged during the mid-eighteenth century when what is now called the modern period was in its relative infancy. It resulted from the decline of the European feudal monarchies and aristocracies, and the gradual ascent of liberal democratic systems. Ever since, the idea of a nation-state has had a tremendous hold on the affairs of the world and on the imagination of the individual; so much so that it is almost inconceivable now to think of the world without nation-states. Currently represented at the United Nations are 191 nations, each with its own national flag, anthem, government, and army. These independent sovereign states with demarcated geographical boundaries and distinct national identities carry out vital functions affecting the political, economic, social, cultural, and educational lives of their citizens. Nationalism is undeniably a force to be reckoned with. It is at once a facilitating force that brings people of a nation together and a debilitating force that pulls people of different nations apart.

The forces of nationalism and nation-states are now being severely challenged by the twin processes of economic and cultural globalization. As the *Human Development Report* (1999) by the United Nations points out, globalization is changing the world landscape in three distinct ways. One, Shrinking space: People's lives are affected by events on the other side of the globe, often by events that they do not even know about, much less control. Two, Shrinking time: Markets and technologies operate at a tremendous speed, with what happens in a far flung place affecting people's lives far away. Three, Disappearing borders: National borders are breaking down, facilitating movement of not only trade and capital goods but also ideas, norms, cultures, and values.

The impact of cultural globalization on nation-states is astounding. As the UN report states (1999: 33):

> Contacts between people and their cultures – their ideas, their values, their way of life – have been growing and deepening in unprecedented ways.

Cultural globalization is shaping the global flows of cultural capital, interested knowledge, and identity formation. Cultures are in closer contact now than ever before, and are influencing each other in complex and complicated ways. This development is creating a global cultural consciousness, and along with it, creative and chaotic tensions that both unite and divide people (see Kumaravadivelu 2008 for more details).

The impact of economic globalization on nation-states is even more astounding. Globalization of capital, labor markets, and trade is having an unfailing and unstoppable effect on the production, distribution and consumption of goods. More than ever, the global society is linked to global economic growth spurred by the increased consumption of goods. As Joel Spring (2007: 250) astutely observes:

> this basic value of the industrial-consumption paradigm cuts across religious and political lines. Hindus, Moslems, Christians, Confucianists, pagans, dictatorships, communists, welfare socialists, representative democracies, monarchies, and authoritarian states all embrace the consumer model.

Problems and solutions facing these global transactions go beyond the level of nation-states. As a consequence, supranational economic institutions such as the World Trade Organization, the World Bank, and the International Monetary Fund exercise extraordinary powers over sovereign nations. As sociologists Michael Hardt and Antonio Negri (2003: 109) rightly point out:

> the era of globalization has not brought the end of the nation-state – nation-states still fulfill extremely important functions in the establishment and regulation of economic, political, and cultural norms – but nation-states have indeed been displaced from the position of sovereign authority.

Echoing a similar sentiment, and citing Benedict Anderson, historian Eric Hobsbawm observes (2007: 88):

> the crucial document of twenty-first century identity is not the nation-state's birth certificate, but the document of international identity – the passport.

In short, the idea of a nation-state that was closely associated with the modern period has been weakened largely because of postmodern developments.

1.1.2 The Postmodern Perspective

There is widespread agreement that we all live in a postmodern world. There is, however, no consensus about the meaning of the term "postmodern" because it is used by various scholars in various disciplines for various purposes. For language teachers and teacher educators, the postmodern perspective offers a path to understanding the status of knowledge, and to understanding the concept of Self (see Chapter 4 for additional note).

French sociologist Jean-Francois Lyotard (1989), in his seminal book *The Postmodern Condition: A Report on Knowledge*, draws insightful distinctions between modernism and postmodernism. To paraphrase his thoughts, modernism looked at scientific knowledge as well as human condition in simplistic terms. It was preoccupied with finding one coherent, overarching truth that could serve as a master key to unlock the conditions of knowledge, and to uncover the conversations about it. It was considered possible to incorporate all forms of knowledge into that one grand narrative. As Lyotard (1989: xxiii) states, modernism sought its legitimacy by making

> explicit appeal to some grand narrative, such as dialectics of the Spirit, the hermeneutics of meaning, the emancipation of the rational or working subject, or the creation of wealth.

Unlike modernism, postmodernism rejects meta-narratives. It acknowledges complexity. It celebrates diversity. As a result, instead of looking for one unifying truth, it recognizes a multiplicity of narratives. Paul Cilliers neatly summarizes Lyotard's position on postmodernism (1998: 114):

> Different groups (institutions, disciplines, communities) tell different stories about what they know and what they do. Their knowledge does not take the form of a logically structured and complete whole, but rather takes the form of narratives that are instrumental in allowing them to achieve their goals and to make sense of what they are doing. Since these narratives are local, they cannot be linked to form a grand narrative which unifies all knowledge.

In other words, postmodernism celebrates difference, challenges hegemonies, and seeks alternative forms of expression and interpretation. It actively seeks to deconstruct metadiscourses by posing questions at the boundaries of ideology, power, knowledge, class, race, and gender.

Yet another aspect of postmodernism relates to its view on individual identity, i.e., the sense of Self. During the days of modernity, the individual's life was largely conditioned by unquestioned and unchanging societal norms. More than anything else, the individual's identity was inseparably tied to that of the family and community. Everybody had a clearly delineated, hierarchically determined place under the sun. And, they were expected to remain there. While some adjustments were allowed, individuals encountered a totalized concept of identity within which they had to find their personal meaning of life. With socially accepted limitations imposed on them, individuals had very little meaningful choice outside the characteristics of birth and ethnic origin. In other words, the "modern" Self was more externally conditioned than internally constructed.

Postmodernism, on the other hand, treats individual identity as something that is continually constructed by the individual on an on-going basis. It sees identity as fragmented, not unified; multiple, not singular; expansive, not bounded. It confers on the individual a degree of agency in determining a sense of Self. As Kumaravadivelu (2008: 144) concludes, according to the postmodern view,

> identity formation is conditioned not merely by inherited traditions such as culture, or by external factors such as history, or by ideological constructs such as power, but also by the individual's ability and willingness to exercise agency and to make independent decisions.

Postmodern thoughts on the status of knowledge, the concept of Self and the exercise of agency are all clearly echoed in postcolonial perspectives as well.

1.1.3 The Postcolonial Perspective

In preparing student teachers to get ready to face the challenges posed by postnational and postmodern developments, language teacher educators, particularly those dealing with languages that have both global and colonial characteristics such as English, French, and Spanish, bear a special responsibility. Consider English. It has certainly become the world's *lingua franca*, the language of choice for international communication. Several scholars and writers have triumphantly characterized it as much more than a language for international communication. Because of its association with global economy, it is deemed to be "the natural choice for progress" (Crystal 1997: 75) for individuals as well as nations. It is credited with

> redefining national and individual identities worldwide; shifting political fault lines; creating new global patterns of wealth and social exclusion; and suggesting new notions of human rights and responsibilities of citizenship.
>
> *(Graddol 2006: 12)*

Furthermore, global English (or Globish) is linked not only to the cultural identities of its users but also to fundamental human values such as freedom.

> For as long as the peoples of the world wish to express themselves in terms of ideas like "freedom", "individuality" and "originality", and for as long as there are generations of the world's school children versed in Shakespeare, The Simpsons, the Declaration of Independence, and the Bible, Globish will remain the means by which an educated minority of the planet communicates.
>
> *(McCrum 2010: 285)*

The triumphant statements can hardly hide the fact that English is not only a language of globality but is also a language of coloniality. Some scholars say, English just happened to be in the right place at the right time (Crystal 1997); others say, it rode on the back of colonialism (Pennycook 1998). Several others highlight its insidious nature of linguistic imperialism (Phillipson 1992), its imperial character that still lingers (Kumaravadivelu 2006a), and its encounters with different forms of resistance (Canagarajah 1999).

From the perspective of postcolonial thoughts, we can easily see how the globalized English Language Teaching (ELT) enterprise has four overlapping dimensions: scholastic, linguistic, cultural and economic (Kumaravadivelu, 2003a). The scholastic dimension shows how the West has furthered its own vested interests by propagating western knowledge and by belittling local knowledge about language learning, teaching, and teacher education. The linguistic dimension reveals how the knowledge and use of local language(s) were made irrelevant for purposes of learning and teaching English worldwide. The cultural dimension aligns the teaching of English language with the teaching of western culture in order to develop cultural assimilative tendencies among L2 learners. These three dimensions are linked to an economic dimension aimed at job and wealth creation benefitting the economy of English speaking countries through a worldwide ELT industry.

Recently, the linguistic and cultural domination of English as a global language has come under severe scrutiny partly because of the process of globalization that has resulted in greater contacts between people of different cultures, leading to a better awareness of each other's values and visions, and to a firmer resolve to preserve and protect one's own linguistic and cultural heritage. There is now a greater awareness that the nature of agency in language teacher education is to a large extent related to the coloniality of the English language mentioned earlier. As a result, there have been attempts by political leaders as well as professional organizations in various parts of the world to "sanitize" the English language from its cultural and political baggage, and focus instead on its instrumental value for international and intercultural communication. For instance, applied linguists in the Middle East have formed professional organizations to promote English language education in ways that best serve the sociopolitical, sociocultural and socioeconomic interests of the Islamic world. In addition, it has become increasingly apparent that the non-English speaking world learns and uses the English language more for purposes of communication than for purposes of cultural identity formation (see Chapter 3, section 3.2. for details).

The linguistic and cultural sensitivities triggered by cultural globalization have prompted the English language teaching community to try to make a meaningful shift in policies and programs, and methods and materials governing English language teaching and teacher education. There is also a growing realization that in order to make any meaningful shift, we need to first go beyond the transmission models of teacher education.

1.1.4 The Post-transmission Perspective

Most traditional ways of teaching and teacher education are considered to follow what is called transmission approaches because they seek to transmit a set of pre-determined, pre-selected and pre-sequenced bodies of knowledge from teacher educators to student teachers. These approaches or models have several characteristics in common. First, they often limit the role of teacher educators to that of conduits who pass on easily digestible bits and pieces of personal and professional knowledge to student teachers. Second, they entail a master-pupil relationship in which student teachers are expected to learn some of their master teacher's pedagogic knowledge and skills, and then try to apply them in their classrooms. Third, they rarely enable or encourage student teachers to construct their own visions and versions of teaching. Fourth, they are essentially top-down approaches that depend on externally produced and expert generated professional knowledge to influence teacher behavior. Finally, they create a debilitating dichotomy between the expert and the teacher, that is, experts are expected to produce knowledge, and teachers are expected to consume knowledge.

Given the five characteristics outlined above, transmission models generally produce teachers who also end up playing the role of a conduit. That is, they become passive technicians channeling the flow of information from one end of the educational spectrum (i.e., experts) to the other (i.e., learners), without in any significant way altering the content of information. Their primary goal is to help their learners comprehend and eventually master content knowledge. In order to achieve that goal, teachers usually rely on the theoretical principles and instructional strategies handed down to them, seldom seriously questioning their validity or relevance to specific learning and teaching contexts that they find themselves in. More often than not, their success as classroom teachers is measured in terms of how closely they adhere to the professional knowledge base transmitted to them, and how effectively they transmit that knowledge base to their learners. While there are eminent exceptions, most traditional teacher education programs fall under this category.

The post-transmission perspective takes a substantially different view of what teachers do in their classrooms, and how they learn to do it. It mainly derives its orientation from recent explorations on teacher cognition, teacher beliefs and other related matters. As Karen Johnson (2006: 239) explains, research findings depict L2 teacher learning

> as normative and lifelong, as emerging out of and through experiences in social contexts: as learners in classrooms and schools, as participants in professional teacher education programs, and later as teachers in the settings where they work. It describes L2 teacher learning as socially negotiated and contingent on knowledge of self, students, subject matter, curricula, and setting. It shows L2 teachers as users and creators of legitimate forms of knowledge who make decisions about how best to teach their L2 students within complex socially, culturally, and historically situated contexts.

What is, therefore, advocated is a judicious combination of cognitive and sociocultural orientations to teacher learning.

The post-transmission perspective seeks to restructure teacher preparation so that it transcends the limitations of transmission models. In doing so, it expects teachers to play the role of reflective practitioners who deeply think about the principles, practices and processes of classroom instruction and bring to their task a considerable degree of creativity, artistry, and context sensitivity. Aiming even further, the post-transmission perspective anticipates teachers to play the role of transformative intellectuals who strive not only for academic advancement but also for personal transformation, both for themselves and for their learners. What it entails is that teacher education needs to pay attention to broader historical, political, social, cultural, and educational factors that impact on teaching. Thus, any serious attempt to move from transmission to post-transmission (Kumaravadivelu 2001: 552)

> must take into account the importance of recognizing teachers' voices and visions, the imperatives of developing their critical capabilities, and the prudence of achieving both of these through a dialogic construction of meaning.

In short, the post-transmission perspective seeks to transform an information-oriented teacher education model into an inquiry-oriented one, with the ultimate goal of producing self-directing and self-determining individuals. In the specific context of L2 teaching and teacher education, transcending the limitations of transmission models also means going beyond the concept of method.

1.1.5 The Postmethod Perspective

The top-down nature of transmission models of teacher education is closely related to the limitations of the concept of method both in general education and in L2 education. General educationists have persistently drawn our attention to what they call "methods fetish" (Bartolome 1994). In fact, they have called for

> an antimethods pedagogy that refuses to be enslaved by the rigidity of models and methodological paradigms.
>
> *(Macedo 1994: 8)*

They see methods as the main source that sustains the dichotomy between theory and practice, between production and consumption of knowledge. Summing up the currently prevailing view, Cochran-Smith and Zeichner (2005: 15) suggest that methods courses must be

> seen as complex and unique sites in which instructors work simultaneously with prospective teachers' beliefs, teaching practices, and creation of identities.

In the field of English language teaching (ELT), there has been a steady stream of critical thoughts on the limitations of the concept of method (Pennycook 1989,

Prabhu 1990, Allwright 1991). The criticism is many-fold. Crucially, as Pennycook (1989: 589–90) has pointed out, the concept of method "reflects a particular view of the world and is articulated in the interests of unequal power relationships" between the expert and the teacher. Besides, as I have argued (Kumaravadivelu 1994), language teaching methods are based on idealized concepts geared towards idealized contexts. Since language learning and teaching needs, wants and situations are unpredictably numerous, no idealized method can visualize all the variables in advance in order to provide situation-specific suggestions that practicing teachers need to tackle the challenges they confront in the practice of their everyday teaching. As a predominantly top-down exercise, the conception and construction of methods have been largely guided by a one-size-fits-all-cookie-cutter approach that assumes a common clientele with common goals. These and other critical thoughts have created what I have called the postmethod condition.

The postmethod condition signifies several possibilities for redefining the top-down character of L2 teacher education. First and foremost, it signifies a search for an alternative to method rather than an alternative method. We now know that there is no best method out there, that a futile search for one will only drive us to continually recycle and repackage the same old ideas, and that nothing short of breaking the cycle can salvage the situation. Secondly, the postmethod condition signifies teacher autonomy. It recognizes the teachers' potential to know not only how to teach but also know how to act autonomously within the academic and administrative constraints imposed by institutions, curricula and textbooks. Finally, the postmethod condition signifies principled pragmatism. It is based on the pragmatics of pedagogy (Widdowson 1990: 30) where

> the relationship between theory and practice, ideas and their actualization, can only be realized within the domain of application, that is, through the immediate activity of teaching.

Principled pragmatism thus focuses on how classroom learning can be shaped and managed by teachers as a result of informed teaching and critical appraisal.

Overall, then, the postmethod perspective seeks to equip student teachers with the knowledge, skill, attitude, and autonomy necessary to devise for themselves a systematic, coherent, and relevant theory of practice (Kumaravadivelu 1994). It promotes the ability of teachers to know how to develop a reflective approach to their own teaching, how to analyze and evaluate their own teaching practice, how to initiate change in their classroom and how to monitor the effects of such changes. That is why postmethod pedagogy has been characterized as

> a compelling idea that emphasizes greater judgment from teachers in each context and a better match between the means and ends.
>
> *(Crabbe 2003: 16)*

The central goal is to transform classroom practitioners into strategic teachers and strategic researchers. It is in this critical sense that the postmethod perspective

> goes beyond the abandonment of the quest for a best method to a fundamental redefinition of method itself, strongly advocating a shift in power from theorisers to practitioners.
>
> *(Murray 2009: 23)*

To conclude this section, the five global perspectives—postnational, postmodern, postcolonial, post-transmission, and postmethod—offer insights that are useful and useable for designing language teacher education for a global society. The postnational perspective demands that we pay attention to global educational and economic flows without at the same time ignoring local linguistic and cultural sensitivities. The postmodern perspective insists that we consider multiple forms of knowledge systems as well as diverse practices of identity formation. The postcolonial perspective alerts us to the scholastic, linguistic, cultural, and economic dimensions of colonial representations that are ever present in educational enterprises. The post-transmission perspective challenges us to visualize inquiry-oriented teacher education programs that are transformative in nature. Finally, the postmethod perspective necessitates the empowerment of classroom practitioners as strategic thinkers and strategic teachers capable of theorizing from their classrooms.

The five global perspectives are deeply interconnected and must be taken together if we are serious about designing comprehensive teacher preparation programs. These perspectives are symbiotically related to a set of operating principles that have the potential to govern the processes and practices of L2 teacher education.

1.2 Operating Principles

The term *operating principles* generally refers to a set of core tenets that define the way a model, a system, or a corporation operates. At a conceptual level, they function like an anchor upon which constitutive elements of a larger unit are affixed together in a coherent manner. At a practical level, they provide the direction and support required to translate certain beliefs, values, and expectations into actionable plans and measurable outcomes.

To my knowledge, the concept of method has long been used as the only overarching operating principle in L2 teaching and teacher education. It has guided the form and function of almost all conceivable components of language pedagogy including curriculum design, syllabus specifications, materials preparation, instructional strategies, and testing techniques. During the 1960s and '70s, the theoretical principles and classroom practices associated with audiolingual method governed all aspects of L2 teaching and teacher education. Since the 1980s, the communicative method of language teaching has been instrumental in spawning several books on communicative grammar, curriculum, syllabus, materials, testing, etc.

The widespread dissatisfaction with the concept of method, discussed earlier, resulted in the postmethod condition which necessitated a search for a new set of operating principles. As part of postmethod pedagogy, I have proposed three parameters, which can function as operating principles for language teacher education as well. They are particularity, practicality, and possibility.

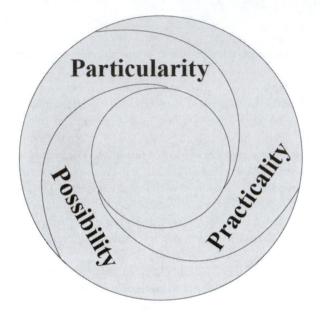

These principles:

> have the potential to offer the necessary conceptualization and contextualization based on the educational, cultural, social, and political imperatives of language learning, teaching, and teacher education. In addition, they offer a pattern that connects the roles of learners, teachers, and teacher educators, promising a relationship that is symbiotic and a result that is synergistic.
>
> *(Kumaravadivelu 2001: 557)*

That is, they interweave and interact with each other in a synergic relationship where the whole is much more than the sum of its parts. Drawing from my earlier work (Kumaravadivelu 2001, 2003b, 2006b), I give below a brief explanation of each of them.

1.2.1 The Principle of Particularity

The principle of particularity is founded on the hermeneutic philosophy of *situational understanding,* which claims that a meaningful pedagogy must be constructed on a holistic interpretation of particular situations, and that it can be improved only by improving those particular situations. Therefore, language teaching and teacher education programs

> must be sensitive to a particular group of teachers teaching a particular group of learners pursuing a particular set of goals within a particular institutional context embedded in a particular sociocultural mileu.
>
> *(Kumaravadivelu 2001: 538)*

The unmistakable emphasis here is on local exigencies and lived experiences. Pedagogies that ignore them will ultimately prove to be

> so disturbing for those affected by them – so threatening to their belief systems – that hostility is aroused and learning becomes impossible.
>
> *(Coleman 1996: 11)*

Any teacher education program must therefore be sensitive to the local individual, institutional, social, and cultural contexts in which learning and teaching take place; if not, it will soon become ineffective and irrelevant. Taking local resources and local constraints into serious consideration, teacher educators need to help present and prospective teachers develop the knowledge and skill necessary to, either individually or collectively, assess the local needs, observe their teaching acts, evaluate their outcomes, identify problems, and find solutions. Such a continual cycle of observation, reflection, and action must be firmly planted in ground reality. Since the particular is so deeply embedded in the practical, and cannot be delinked from it, the principle of particularity is intertwined with the principle of practicality.

1.2.2 The Principle of Practicality

The principle of practicality relates broadly to the relationship between theory and practice, and narrowly to the teachers' skill in monitoring their own teaching effectiveness. There is a harmful dichotomy between theory and practice, between the role of the theorist and the role of the teacher in producing and using pedagogic knowledge. The principle of practicality aims to break the established division of labor between the theorist and the teacher, between the producer and consumer of knowledge. Such an artificial division leaves very little room for self-conceptualization and self-construction of pedagogic knowledge on the part of the teacher. It is rather apparent that pedagogic knowledge, to have any local relevance, must emerge from the practice of everyday teaching. This is something that teachers themselves have to explore; only then can they theorize from practice (see Chapters 5 and 6 for more).

The objective of enabling teachers to theorize from practice cannot be achieved simply by asking them to put into practice professional theories proposed by others. It can be achieved only by instituting a teacher preparation program that will develop in them the knowledge and skill, attitude and autonomy necessary to construct their own context-sensitive theory of practice. A central role of teacher education, therefore, is to provide prospective and practicing teachers with adequate tools for classroom observation and pedagogic exploration that views teaching not merely as a mechanism for maximizing learning opportunities in the classroom but also as a means for understanding and transforming learner and teacher possibilities in and outside the classroom (see Chapter 5 for an extended discussion). In this sense, the principle of practicality merges with the principle of possibility.

1.2.3 The Principle of Possibility

The principle of possibility is derived mainly from critical pedagogy advocated by the Brazilian educational thinker Paulo Freire and his followers. Critical pedagogists see pedagogy, any pedagogy, as effectively used by vested interests as an instrument to create and sustain social inequalities. As Joe Kincheloe (2009: 34) puts it in a recent article, critical pedagogists construct their

> philosophical foundation on notions of empowered, professionalized teachers working to cultivate the intellect and enhance the socioeconomic mobility of students by larger sociocultural and political impulses. Teachers in a critical pedagogy conduct research into these social and educational dynamics, design curricula around multiple macro-knowledges of education and the contexts in which it operates and the micro-situations in which their students find themselves in their communities and their schools.

They see classroom reality as socially constructed and historically determined. What is therefore required to counter the social and historical forces that strive to maintain its power structure is a pedagogy of possibility that empowers participants to critically appropriate forms of knowledge outside of their immediate experience.

Extending Freirean thoughts to language education and language teacher education, critical discourse analysts focus on the role of critical language awareness in developing sociopolitical consciousness. They argue that language learners and teachers can contest practices of domination only by making the relationship between language and power explicit. They believe that critical language awareness

> can lead to reflexive analysis of practices of domination implicit in the transmission and learning of academic discourse, and the engagement of learners in the struggle to contest and change such practices.
>
> *(Fairclough 1995: 222)*

They stress the need for teachers to develop theories and practices that are relevant to the individual and collective experiences that participants bring to the classroom setting. These experiences have the potential to shape classroom events and activities not anticipated by policy planners, curriculum designers, or textbook producers.

The principle of possibility is also treating the experiences gained from the language classroom as resources for individual identity formation. More than any other educational experience, language use and learning purpose offer singular opportunities for a continual quest for subjectivity and self-identity. As Chris Weeden (1997: 21) rightly points out,

> language is the place where actual and possible forms of social organization and their likely social and political consequences are defined and contested. Yet it is also the place where our sense of ourselves, our subjectivity, is constructed.

Therefore, it makes eminent sense to use the language learning experience as an instrument for developing sociocultural consciousness.

This quest for self-identity assumes greater importance now more than ever because of the impact of economic and cultural globalization. Therefore,

> a critical pedagogy of the global must be able to reckon with the fundamental transformations of consciousness, experience, and identity that are central to the shift to the historical condition of globality.
>
> *(De Lissovoy 2009: 191)*

Given the demands and expectations of the globalized environment, language teacher educators are faced with the task of helping present and prospective teachers become aware of how they are positioned in various historical, social, and institutional contexts, and also become aware of the possibilities and strategies for transgressing the artificial boundaries imposed upon them by vested interests. A teacher education program wedded to the principle of possibility has to help teachers face the challenge of moving beyond well-entrenched discourses and practices that they have come to heavily rely upon.

To sum up this section, the principle of particularity opposes pre-selected principles and procedures that are aimed at producing predetermined goals and objectives; instead, it favors the advancement of context-sensitive teaching and teacher education programs based on a true understanding of local linguistic, sociocultural and political particularities. The principle of practicality opposes the debilitating dichotomy between theorists and teachers; instead, it favors teacher education programs that enable teachers to theorize from their practice and practice what they theorize. The principle of possibility opposes language teacher education programs that merely transmit a (dead?) body of content knowledge; instead, it favors those that raise sociopolitical consciousness among all the participants so that they can form and transform their personal and social identity.

The principles of particularity, practicality, and possibility thus constitute the operating principles needed for constructing a viable teacher education program. These principles along with the five global perspectives discussed earlier have the potential to guide us in designing a coherent, comprehensive teacher education program that is transformative in nature. Together, they demand that we re-view and re-vision language teacher education in order to come up with a set of new and challenging priorities.

1.3 Challenging Priorities

To put it in a nutshell, what the global perspectives and the operating principles stipulate we must do is to visualize a teacher education program that seeks to help present and prospective teachers focus

- more on the production of personal knowledge than on the application of received wisdom, so that their teaching draws upon their learned expertise as well as lived experience;
- more on acceleration of agency than on acceptance of authority, so that they can have the freedom and flexibility they deserve and desire;
- more on teacher research with local touch than on expert research with global reach, so that what they do in the classroom meets local needs, wants, and lacks;
- more on becoming transformative intellectuals than on being passive technicians, so that they can carry out their social obligations along with their pedagogic obligations; and
- more on mastering the teaching model than on modeling the master teacher, so that they develop the competence and the confidence necessary to cope with the unknown and the unexpected.

The perspectives, principles and priorities offer conceptual underpinnings that facilitate the designing of a coherent and comprehensive model of language teacher education.

1.4 Designing KARDS

One of the inherent weaknesses of the traditional approaches to L2 teacher education is the sequential course offerings that focus on one discrete course after another on content areas that are considered important. At present, most of the L2 teacher education programs offer their clients (i.e., prospective teachers) a series of independent, stand-alone courses in areas such as linguistic theories, second language acquisition, pedagogic grammar, methods, curriculum, and testing, usually ending with a capstone course in practicum or practice teaching. Each class is, of course, clearly and carefully delineated with its own general goals and specific objectives. Based on faculty advisement, prospective teachers take these classes taught by different teacher educators, do their best to acquire content knowledge, get good grades, and after completing the required number of classes, graduate. And then they are expected to teach happily ever after. Such a rigidly formulated set of courses rarely presents a holistic picture of learning, teaching, and teacher development, and it is generally left to student teachers to see "the pattern that connects." This is the general scenario that plays out everywhere, although there may be variations on the theme.

The teacher education model I am proposing is modular in nature. It attempts to do away with the idea of a linear, discrete, additive, and compartmentalized character of teacher education. Instead, it aims at providing a cyclical, integrated, interactive, multidirectional and multidimensional focus for it. A modular approach lends itself to an identification and integration of componential modules that function as a whole. Each identified module has a specific purpose but fulfills its purpose by drawing sustenance from others. Thus, a modular model constitutes a network of mutually reinforcing sub-systems that are engaged in a dialectical interplay resulting in a holistic learning and teaching environment.

The modular model I am elaborating on in the following pages is structured in the form of five constituent modules—Knowing, Analyzing, Recognizing, Doing and Seeing (KARDS). In identifying these components, I have kept in mind what teachers have to basically do in order to become self-determining and self-transforming individuals. They have to (a) develop their professional, procedural and personal knowledge base; (b) analyze learner needs, motivation, and autonomy; (c) recognize their own identities, beliefs and values; (d) perform teaching, theorizing and dialogizing; and (e) monitor their own teaching acts. Any viable teacher education program, then, must promote the conditions and capabilities necessary for present and prospective teachers to know, to analyze, to recognize, to do, and to see learning, teaching, and teacher development. It must help them to develop a holistic understanding of what happens in their classroom, so that, eventually, they will be able to theorize from practice and practice what they theorize.

1.5 In Closing

I began this chapter highlighting the need for a cogent, coherent and comprehensive model for L2 teacher education that could help us get to grips with the educational complexity that has become the hallmark of our globalized knowledge society. Any such model, I argued, must be erected on the twin pillars of global perspectives, and operating principles. I presented five global perspectives—postnational, postmodern, postcolonial, post-transmission, and postmethod—that emerge from various disciplines in the humanities and social sciences. I pointed out that these global perspectives are symbiotically connected to the principles of particularity, practicality, and possibility. I further contended that these principles can function as operating principles underpinning the exploration and execution of a viable L2 teacher education program.

The global perspectives and the operating principles warrant a thorough and thoughtful re-view and re-vision of our priorities in terms of the content and con-duct of L2 teacher education. Informed by the global perspectives, organizing principles, and challenging priorities, I proposed a modular model consisting of five componential modules: Knowing, Analyzing, Recognizing, Doing, and Seeing. I have claimed that the modular model, with its cyclical, interactive, and integrative nature, addresses some of the drawbacks associated with traditional approaches to L2 teacher education and, thus, has the potential to help us move away from transmission and towards transformation. In the following chapters, I present a detailed treatment of each of the modules.

Rapid Reader Response

Write a quick response to the following questions. Form small groups, share your thoughts and discuss them with other members of the group.

1   What is the one big point you learned from this chapter?
2   What is the one main unanswered question you leave the chapter with?
3   What is the one surprising idea or concept you encountered in this chapter?
4   What is the one example of terminology or concept you do not fully understand?

Reflective Tasks

Task 1.1 Posing the Right Questions

T1.1.1 Think about the statement made by American educationists Marilyn Cochran-Smith and Kenneth Zeichner: "education and teacher education are social institutions that pose moral, ethical, social, philosophical, and ideological questions." Do you agree or disagree that it is the responsibility of educational institutions to pose questions of such a nature? What are your reasons?

T1.1.2 What kinds of moral, ethical, social, philosophical, or ideological questions do (or should) educational institutions pose?

T1.1.3 Recall your days at school and/or college. Provide an example of a moral or ethical or social question that your educational institute posed. How did you resolve the question? How did your classmates and/or your teacher(s) assist you in resolving the question? To what extent did the school/college prepare you to identify and resolve the issue?

Task 1.2 Facing the New Global Context

T1.2.1 The report on *Transforming Teacher Education* asserts: "Notwithstanding their origins, commonalities and differences, all systems of teacher preparation have to rethink their core assumptions and processes in the new global context" (2008: 14). What do you think are the "assumptions and processes" that govern the system of teacher preparation that you are familiar with?

T1.2.2 Does "the new global context" really warrant a "rethink" of the "assumptions and processes" that you have identified? If yes, why? If not, why not?

T1.2.3 If you were vested with necessary authority, what two fundamental changes would you make to the existing "systems of teacher preparation," and why?

Exploratory Project

Project 1.1 Preparing to Meet the Brave New World

The general goal of this project is to help you explore and understand the fundamental character of a graduate level teacher preparation program you are currently associated with.

P1.1.1 Consult your University catalog in which departments and programs are listed along with course requirements. Take a close look at the overall curriculum designed specifically for your teacher education program. Study the brief description of the general goals, specific objectives and learning outcomes for each of the core courses and electives.

P1.1.2 What are the characteristic features of the curriculum that appear to fit in with the essentials of a transmission model of teacher education? (See section 1.1.4 for details.)

P1.1.3 What are the characteristic features of the curriculum that appear to fit in with the essentials of a post-transmission model of teacher education? (See section 1.1.4 for details.)

P1.1.4 What are the possible operating principles that, according to you, might have informed the overall goals and objectives of your teacher education program?

P1.1.5 Based on your curricular analysis, and your classroom experience (this might include your exposure to class expectations, instructional strategies, course assignments, philosophical orientations of your professors, and any other relevant information), discuss the extent to which your teacher education program seeks to develop in you the knowledge, skill, and disposition necessary to become autonomous individuals capable of functioning in a globalized educational context.

2

KNOWING

People disparage knowing and the intellectual life, and urge doing. I am content with knowing, if only I could know.

(Ralph Waldo Emerson 1903: 84)

2.0 Introduction

This module is named *knowing* instead of *knowledge*. The emphasis here is more on the ways of knowing than on the body of knowledge. Knowing is a process; knowledge is a product. Clearly, the two are connected, and might even be considered inseparable. However, knowing is deemed to have greater significance than knowledge. That is why scientists and philosophers alike have persistently challenged us to reflect on the meaning of knowing. Among them are John Dewey, an educator and philosopher of education, and Michael Polanyi, a scientist and philosopher of science.

John Dewey considers the term *knowledge* to be problematic particularly when it is connected to constructs such as learning, and intelligence. It is

> too wide and vague to be a *name* of anything in particular. The butterfly "knows" how to mate, presumably without learning; the dog "knows" its master through learning; man "knows" through learning how to do an immense number of things in the way of arts or abilities; he also "knows" physics, and "knows" mathematics; he knows *that*, *what*, and *how*.
>
> *(Dewey & Bentley 1949: 194, all original emphasis)*

Skeptical of *knowledge*, Dewey argues for the centrality of *knowing* in learning as well as in life. As Deron Boyles (2006: 64) explains it,

knowing, knowledge, and intelligence are distinct for Dewey. Knowing is a
process of inquiry (specific instances of applying oneself to solving problems);
knowledge constitutes the stable outcomes of inquiry; and intelligence is the
result of developing and accumulating capabilities to act (that is, to inquire) in
specific ways.

For Dewey, knowing is not confined to some abstract thinking that takes
place somewhere in the human mind. On the contrary, it is very much rooted in
the personal activity of the knower. It is "literally something which we do"
(Dewey 1916: 367). It is about reflection and action. It is about the result of the
dialectical relationship between reflection and action. That is to say, reflection
informs action, and action informs reflection. There is reciprocal effort. There is
mutual benefit.

Polanyi's ideas about knowing are not very different. Even as a scientist, he
articulates a healthy skepticism about the notions of objectivity, truth, and knowledge
normally associated with science and scientific method. He questions the common
belief that science is somehow value-free. He argues that informed guesses, hunches,
and imaginings that are part of human creativity should also be valued even though
we may not be able to state them in propositional terms acceptable to science. He
also maintains that "we can know more than we can tell" (1966: 4). He calls this
tacit knowledge. This tacit form of knowing is rather personal and is embedded in the
principle of particularity (cf: section 1.2.2. in Chapter 1). That is to say, it varies
from individual to individual, from context to context. Therefore, it may not have
universal validity.

For Polanyi, then, knowing is "the personal participation of the knower in all
acts of understanding" (1958: vii). It entails "a passionate contribution of the person
knowing what is being known" (p. viii). It also implies "an ontology of the mind"
(p. 264); that is to say, a person is "entitled to shape his knowing according his own
judgment, unspecifiably" (p. 264). Polanyi's emphasis on the individual knower's
personal judgment does not mean "anything goes." Shaping one's knowing is not
just a matter of one's subjective judgment; it is also a mark of one's intellectual
commitment—a commitment to understand the dialectical relationship between
awareness and action, between theoretical knowledge and practical wisdom.

The idea of knowing espoused by Dewey and Polanyi has immense relevance to
teaching and teacher education. We can learn from them about the importance of,
and the need for, paying attention to the amalgamation of personal reflection and
action which result in a deeper understanding of what might constitute teacher
knowledge.

How teachers and teacher educators develop this understanding has long been a
subject of inquiry in general education. In fact, the inquiry is so wide and deep that
one comes across a dizzying display of terms and concepts to refer to this understanding. At a very broad level, we find the term *teacher knowledge* used as an
umbrella term to cover teachers' theoretical and practical knowledge as well as their

dispositions, beliefs, and values. Similarly, we also find the terms *content knowledge, subject matter knowledge, propositional knowledge,* or *disciplinary knowledge* used to refer to facts, theories, and concepts pertaining to a particular academic field.

In addition, there are greatly nuanced treatments of teacher knowledge as well. Correctly identifying teacher knowledge as a "missing paradigm" in the educational research on the content of teaching, Lee Shulman (1986a) first presented a useful analysis in which he divided content knowledge into *disciplinary content knowledge* (i.e., facts, concepts, etc.), *pedagogical content knowledge* (i.e., teaching methods, classroom presentation, etc.), and *curricular knowledge* (i.e., materials, syllabus, etc.). Subsequently he developed finer "categories of knowledge that underlie the teacher understanding needed to promote comprehension among students" (1987: 8). This new category consisted of *general pedagogical knowledge* (broad principles and strategies of classroom management and organization), *curriculum knowledge* (a grasp of the materials and programs that serve as tools of the trade), *pedagogical content knowledge* (content and pedagogy unique to teachers), *knowledge of learners* (their individual characteristics), *knowledge of educational contexts* (group dynamics, the governance and financing of school districts, the character of communities and cultures), and *knowledge of educational ends* (purposes, and values, and philosophical and historical rationale governing them). In proposing such a detailed set of teacher knowledge, Shulman was careful to caution us that "much, if not most, of the proposed knowledge base remains to be discovered, invented, and refined" (p. 12).

Freema Elbaz (1983) proposed yet another concept called *practical knowledge* which she considered as

> the single factor which seems to have the greatest power to carry forward our understanding of the teachers' role.
>
> *(p. 45)*

It encompasses

> teachers' knowledge of subject matter, curriculum, instruction, classroom management, school and community, learning styles, as well as knowledge of their own attitudes, values, beliefs and goals – all shaped by their practical classroom experience. All of these kinds of knowledge, as integrated by the individual teacher in terms of personal values and beliefs and as oriented to her practical situation, will be referred to as "practical knowledge."
>
> *(Ibid.: 5)*

Adding yet another layer, Jean Clandinin and Michael Connelly (1987) suggested the term *personal practical knowledge* because, for them, teacher knowledge constitutes teachers' personal stories and narratives derived from the demands of a particular learning and teaching situation. It is a kind of knowledge carved out of, and shaped by, situations; knowledge that is constructed and reconstructed as we live out our stories and retell and relive them through processes of reflection.

(Clandinin 1992: 125)

Others have used other terms: strategic knowledge, relational knowledge, craft knowledge, case knowledge, situated knowledge. And there are more. As Gary Fenstermacher (1994: 7) rightly points out, the multiple labels and terms

> do not necessarily refer to different types of knowledge. They are, in some ways, like the names we give to people. Each of us has a given (formal) first name, usually a nickname, and often another name that is a family favorite; we may have still other names because of our membership in certain religious or social groups. These names all refer to the same person, although their context of use is different.

In dealing with all these types of knowledge, we should keep an important caveat in mind. It pertains to the limitations of doing research on teacher knowledge. Most of the knowledge-related terms and concepts presented above are mutually defining and largely overlapping, carrying terminological and conceptual ambiguities. As such, they may not survive rigorous scrutiny. From a cognitive perspective, they are all fragmented because it is difficult, almost impossible, to separate one sub-type of knowledge from another sufficiently enough to investigate. From a methodological perspective, we are yet to devise an investigative technique that will help us study what we want to study. Most of the research projects in teacher knowledge have depended on data collection techniques such as interviews, diary studies, case studies, self-reports, think aloud protocols, simulated recall, etc. By analyzing whatever participating teachers say, the researcher has to infer a possible underlying knowledge they might have used for reflection and action. As David Block (2000: 759) points out in another context, what someone says in response to data elicitation are merely "*voices* adopted by research participants in response to the researcher's prompts and questions" (original emphasis).

They should be seen more as

> symptomatic of a particular state of mind and even ephemeral, ongoing social interaction than as a reflection of underlying memory or mental models of particular domains of knowledge and experience.

(Ibid.: 760)

Studies on teacher knowledge, therefore, can at best reveal only partial knowledge.

The plethora of labels and definitions one finds in the literature is a clear indication of the richness of the knowledge base that is now available for analysis and interpretation. But, for the purposes of teacher preparation, I believe we should focus on a set of manageable, and yet meaningful, types of knowledge. Therefore, I consolidate various insights gleaned from the literature, and draw a simple frame of reference consisting of (a) professional knowledge; (b) procedural knowledge; and (c) personal knowledge.

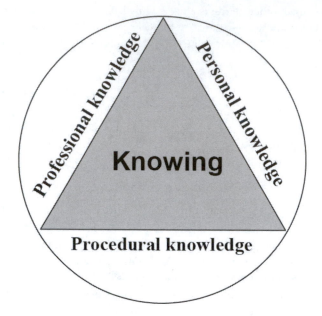

In the following sections, I will outline the nature and scope of these three types of knowledge. I will also try to show how the professional, the procedural, and the personal will position teachers' ways of knowing. It will become clear that the three are closely connected and that they influence each other.

2.1 Professional Knowledge

Professional knowledge is received wisdom that emanates mostly from experts who are engaged in knowledge production in a given discipline. It represents the intellectual content of the discipline, a compilation of facts, theories, and concepts. It is knowledge that is shared by the members of the profession. Teachers acquire professional knowledge from a combination of sources: pre- and in-service training programs, books, journals, conferences, conversations, etc. In the context of L2 teacher education, professional knowledge relates to the fundamental concepts of language, language learning, and language teaching. I give below a synopsis of L2 professional knowledge drawn from the professional literature and presented in Kumaravadivelu (2006b, for expanded descriptions, see the source).

2.1.1 *Knowledge about Language*

Knowledge about language entails knowledge of language as system, language as discourse, and language as ideology. Language as system focuses on the systems and sub-systems of language, how they are systematic and rule-governed. Thus, the phonological system deals with patterns of sound—which sounds can appear word-initially or word-finally, or in what clusters. It also pertains to how certain sound sequences signify certain meanings. The semantic system deals with the meaning of words, how every morpheme—a collection of phonemes arranged in a particular way—expresses a canonical meaning. The syntactic system deals with the rules of grammar, showing how

> the nouns and verbs and adjectives are not just hitched end to end in one long chain, there is some overarching blueprint or plan for the sentence that puts each word in a specific slot.
>
> *(Pinker 1994: 94)*

Understanding the units of language as system with its rules as well as the rules for combination enables L2 learners and users to speak and write in a grammatically acceptable way.

Language as discourse deals with the cohesive nature of connected texts. It denotes the coherent relationship between form, meaning, and the communicative intent within a particular communicative situation, so that language use comes out to be grammatically correct as well as communicatively appropriate. At a broader level, it denotes the interplay between what Halliday (1973) calls the ideational, interpersonal, and textual functions of language. The ideational function represents the expression and experience of the concepts, processes, and objects governing the physical and natural phenomena of the world around us. The interpersonal function deals with the individual's personal relationship with people and the role language plays in it. The textual function refers to the linguistic realizations of the ideational and interpersonal functions enabling the language user to construct coherent texts, spoken or written. Language as discourse, thus, takes a predominantly linguistic approach to understanding the meaning potential of language.

Language as ideology goes beyond formal and discoursal features and takes into consideration the higher order operations of language at the intersection of social, cultural, political, and ideological meanings. It recognizes that most often language is used in a particular way to express a particular point of view to achieve a particular goal. It also recognizes that language is tied to power and domination. It reflects the ideologically grounded perceptions and practices that are shaped by dominant institutional forces, historical processes, and vested interests. It acknowledges that language can be used, misused, and abused to serve narrow political or ideological goals. A critical analysis of language as ideology can also unravel how language is exploited in the service of power.

2.1.2 Knowledge about Language Learning

Knowledge about language learning in institutionalized contexts encompasses theoretical and empirical insights derived from fields such as second language acquisition (SLA), cognitive psychology, and information processing. One way of understanding the insights is by looking at the nature of five major constructs that constitute the input-output chain in language learning and language use: input, intake, intake factors, intake processes, and output.

Input refers to the body of language that is available and accessible to L2 learners. It constitutes the oral and/or written corpus of the target language to which L2 learners are exposed through various sources, and recognized by them as useful and useable for purposes of language learning. Possible sources where learners can get language input include (a) the language that is generally used by competent speakers to speak and write to one another, and the language that is used by various media outlets; (b) the grammatically and lexically simplified language that teachers, textbook writers, and other competent speakers use in and outside the classroom while addressing language learners; and (c) the still developing language of the learners and of their peers with all its linguistically well-formed as well as deviant utterances.

Intake is "what goes in and not what is *available* to go in" (Corder 1967: 165, original emphasis) and as such it constitutes only a portion of the language input that is exposed to learners. It is an abstract entity of learner language that has been fully or partially processed and internalized by learners, and has thus become part of their developing linguistic repertoire, also called interlanguage. Intake is the result of as yet undetermined interaction between input and intake factors mediated by intake processes. It is not directly observable, quantifiable or analyzable because it is a complex cluster of mental representations. Researchers in SLA attempt to decipher intake by collecting and analyzing spoken and written interlanguage produced by learners who are still in the process of developing their L2.

Intake factors, among others, facilitate L2 development. There is no consensus in the field about which and how many factors are involved. A review of SLA literature gives us an idea of what might be considered as facilitating factors. There are individual factors such as age, anxiety, attitude, motivation, extroversion, introversion, and risk-taking. These factors play a crucial role in determining individual success or failure in language learning. There are strategic factors such as learning strategies, communication strategies, and interpretive strategies. These factors provide necessary tools and techniques for effective language learning. There are educational factors such as language policies and language planning put in place by governmental or educational agencies. These factors determine the types and goals of instructional programs made available to L2 learners. Some factors (e.g., individual factors) are internal to learners in the sense that they have a reasonable control over them, while others (e.g., educational factors) are considered external because learners play very little role in shaping them.

Intake processes are cognitive mechanisms that mediate between, and interact with, input data and intake factors. They are mental operations that are specific to language learning as well as those that are required for general problem-solving skills. They govern what goes on in the learner's mind when they attempt to internalize the linguistic system from the available and accessible input data. These processes appear to shape L2 development by helping learners infer the nuances of the linguistic system through a series of mental operations involving hypothesis-formation, hypothesis-testing and hypothesis-confirmation. They seem to combine elements of what psycholinguists have called *analysis* and *control*. The former is connected to language knowledge and the latter to language ability. As learners begin to understand how the L2 system works, and as their mental representations of the system become more structured, they begin to see the relationships between various linguistic categories and concepts. Control is the process that allows learners to

> direct their attention to specific aspects of the environment or a mental representation as problems are solved in real time.
>
> *(Bialystok 2002: 153)*

Output refers to the corpus of utterances which learners actually produce orally or in writing. In addition to well-formed utterances that may have already been structured and restructured, the learner output will contain deviant utterances which cannot be traced to any of the sources of input since they are the result of an interplay between intake factors and intake processes, and they may indicate developmental phases that learners go through.

It is fairly apparent that these five constructs—input, intake, intake factors, intake processes, and output—interact with each other, resulting eventually in successful L2 development. How the variables shape each other, and which cognitive or other mechanisms accelerate or retard the interplay, remain as yet undetermined.

2.1.3 Knowledge about Language Teaching

Knowledge about language teaching has thus far been concerned primarily with knowledge about methods of language teaching. Established methods ranging from Grammar-Translation to Audiolingual to Communicative adhere to one of two basic approaches to language teaching: (a) use through usage or (b) usage through use, where use refers to communicative fluency and usage refers to grammatical accuracy.

The "use through usage" approach is heavily dependent on language as system. Curriculum designers and textbook writers carefully select a set of grammatical structures and vocabulary items, and sequence them according to their perceived difficulty level. Through grammar-focused exercises, teachers are advised to introduce one discrete item at a time and help learners practice until they internalize it. The assumption here is that a continual and conscious attention to linguistic features in the classroom will ultimately lead learners to communicate in the target language outside the class. That is, grammatical competence is deemed to ultimately lead to communicative competence. Language learning, therefore, is considered more intentional than incidental.

The "usage through use" approach is based on the assumption that language learning is more incidental than intentional. A language is best learned when the focus is not on the language; that is, when the learner's attention is focused on understanding, saying, and doing something with language, even if they are not explicitly preoccupied with its formal properties. What is important is the attention learners pay to the process of meaning-making, and getting a message across. Accordingly, curriculum designers and textbook writers develop meaning-oriented, problem-solving tasks and other communication-oriented activities. Teachers are expected to use them to create the conditions necessary for learners to engage in open-ended, meaningful interaction in class. Grammar construction is deemed to take place automatically and eventually.

Embedded in the two basic approaches is the notion of intervention aimed at promoting desired learning outcomes in the classroom. We intervene by modifying the content and style of language input, and by modifying the nature and scope of interactional opportunities. Input modifications may be (a) form-based; (b) meaning-based; or (c) form- and meaning-based. Form-based modifications have almost always been based on the structural properties of the language, whether they relate to grammatical forms or communicative functions. The idea is to draw the learner's attention to the structural properties in order to increase the degree of explicitness required for promoting L2 development. Meaning-based modifications, on the other hand, draw the learner's attention to meaning through communicative tasks such as games or information gap activities. They make sure that necessary grammar is embedded in meaningful contexts. Form- and meaning-based input modifications believe that focusing on both of them is more beneficial than focusing on either one of them. Together, they draw the learner's attention to the interactive nature of form, meaning, and discourse.

Interactional modifications may take place at different levels of sophistication. At a basic level, they are designed to help learners learn to modify their speech phonologically, lexically, and syntactically in order to maximize chances of mutual understanding, and minimize instances of communication breakdown. They also promote conversational exchanges that arise when participants try to accommodate potential or actual problems of understanding, using strategies such as comprehension checks or clarification checks. At another level, interactional modifications deal with interpersonal communication. They refer to the participants' potential to establish and maintain social relationships in interpersonal encounters, and the outcome is measured in terms of personal rapport created in the classroom. At yet another level, interactional modifications focus on ideas and emotions learners bring with them, giving them the freedom to express their views on their life experience both in and outside the classroom. They provide opportunities for increased learner-learner interaction and create and sustain learner motivation in classroom interaction. In short, the first level focuses mostly on the systemic concept, the second mostly on the discoursal context, and the third mostly on the ideological content of language communication.

In sum, professional knowledge directed towards present and prospective teachers in the field of L2 learning and teaching covers theories and practices of language, language learning, and language teaching. It represents a body of accumulated and shared knowledge of the profession even though it may lack universal acceptance. In addition to providing professional knowledge, experts also seek to help teachers with their procedural knowledge.

2.2 Procedural Knowledge

Procedural knowledge is about knowing how to manage classroom learning and teaching. It is about creating and sustaining a classroom environment in which desired learning outcomes are made possible. It is about facilitating the flow of the lesson, channelizing it in the right direction. In short, it is about classroom management.

Research on classroom management has a long tradition in general education. The editors of a recently published *Handbook of Classroom Management* define it as

> the actions teachers take to create an environment that supports and facilitates both academic and social-emotional learning. In other words, classroom management has two distinct purposes: It not only seeks to establish and sustain an orderly environment so students can engage in meaningful academic learning, it also aims to enhance students' social and moral growth.
>
> *(Evertson & Weinstein 2006: 4)*

According to the editors, teachers seek to achieve these two purposes by (a) developing responsive and supportive relationships with and among students; (b) organizing teaching in ways that optimize students' access to learning; (c) using managerial strategies that encourage students' engagement in academic tasks; (d) promoting the development of students' social skills and self-regulation; and (e) using appropriate interventions to assist students with behavior problems.

Historically, general educationists have followed two broad approaches to classroom management: behavioral and ecological. For decades, influenced by behaviorist psychology that emphasized reinforcement and stimulus control, educationists focused narrowly on monitoring and managing students with behavior problems and on taking appropriate disciplinary measures. The emphasis was on rules, rewards, and penalties. The central goal was to maintain an orderly environment so that effective teaching could take place. Later, recognizing that classroom management is far more complex than just controlling student behavior, educationists turned to an ecological approach that stressed the importance of context-specific community building in the classroom. Since the 1980s, the focus of classroom management has shifted from generic teacher traits to classroom-specific management models, from interactions with individual students to management of the class as a group, and from managing behavior to managing learning (Doyle 2006).

One finds echoes of the ecological approach in the principles of classroom management advocated by ELT professionals. In a pioneering article, Dick Allwright (1981: 5) introduced the term *management of language learning* and identified three phases in the practice of it:

> there are things to decide, actions to be taken on the basis of those decisions, and a process of review to feed into future decision-making.

He later argued that managing learning should be the joint endeavor of both the teacher and the learner. Jointly, they have to maintain the conditions necessary for maximizing learning opportunities in the classroom. As he stated elsewhere:

> All are agents. And so, learner behavior could usefully be seen as contributing to lessons by materially affecting the agenda in the classroom, for good or ill.
>
> *(Allwright 2005: 16)*

There are several aspects to the management of classroom language learning, the most important of which are talk management and topic management (Kumaravadivelu 2003b). Talk management mainly involves managing the structure of information exchange, which in turn involves the type of questions asked and responses expected. The information structure in most language classes follows what is called the IRF sequence, that is, the teacher initiates (I), the learner responds (R), and the teacher provides appropriate feedback (F). In most traditional classes where the teacher controls the talk management, the IRF sequence predominates. Such a tradition often limits opportunities for meaningful interaction to take place. To move away from this rigid formula, teachers are advised to ask *referential* questions which seek new information and permit open-ended responses from students, rather than *display* questions which allow teachers and learners only to display a closed set of language use. Teachers can promote genuine conversation if they closely link their talk management with topic management.

Topic management relates to the content of classroom talk. Normally, teachers confine themselves to discussing the topics included in the prescribed textbook. However, going beyond them and encouraging students to initiate topics of their interest is likely to increase their motivation to participate in classroom interaction. Besides, it allows the learners to share their individual perspectives on contemporary topics with the teacher as well as other learners whose lives, and hence perspectives, may differ from theirs. Research shows that there are several advantages to letting learners have partial control over the topic: it can result (a) in the tailoring of the linguistic complexity of the input to the learner's own level; (b) in the creation of better opportunities for negotiating meaning when a communication problem arises; and (c) in the stimulation of more extensive and more complex production of language on the part of the learners (Slimani 1989, Ellis 1992). The teacher, of course, may have to skillfully manage any hot button issues that learners might raise.

Teachers have to be aware that talk and topic management may be influenced by several factors including teaching goals and methods, and learner profiles. A management strategy that aims at passive compliance on the part of the learner may go against the goals of a teaching method that emphasizes active learning and joint production of classroom discourse. A class with learners from diverse linguistic and cultural backgrounds may require management strategies that are sensitive to learners' expectations. In addition, teachers are expected to be knowledgeable about several pedagogic procedures that ease the flow of the lesson. They include (a) when to opt for individual, pair, group or whole class activity; (b) what criteria to follow to form pairs and groups; (c) the length of time they will have to wait after posing a question before rephrasing or redirecting the question to another student; and (d) if and when to allow learners to use their first language in class. A challenging aspect of these and other classroom management strategies is that they are defined and achieved within a specific learning and teaching context, each of which may make differential demands on the teacher.

In spite of the importance, and the challenging nature, of classroom management, there are very few teacher education programs that offer well-organized, hands-on experience in management strategies. It is fair to assume that most teachers develop their procedural knowledge (a) through what Lortie (1975) calls "apprenticeship of observation," that is, teachers have observed classroom teaching for many, many years just by being a student, and may have absorbed certain teaching techniques and management strategies from their teachers; and (b) through trial and error method during their own teaching days. Research shows that learning procedural knowledge along with professional knowledge would be most beneficial for prospective teachers, and that this can easily be done through teaching practicum that includes field experiences, role plays and video analyses (Crookes 2003, Tsui 2003). Research also shows that the lack of procedural knowledge may be a significant factor in teachers' difficulty in applying the professional knowledge gained in teacher education programs to the practice of everyday teaching (Bartels 2006).

To sum up this section, procedural knowledge constitutes knowledge and ability to manage classroom language learning effectively. Appropriate classroom management strategies are necessary for properly directing the flow of learning and teaching. By using such strategies during the early days of a class, teachers can formulate a classroom culture that will set the tone for the rest of the academic year. It is mostly through the effective use of procedural knowledge that teachers send a strong message to their learners as to what kind of classroom climate that they can expect. Classroom management

> with all its complexities, ambiguities, and dilemmas, requires a teacher to go beyond mere control tactics and engage in both critical inquiry, and thoughtful reflection, the hallmarks of reflective practitioners.
>
> *(Larrivee 2006: 984)*

It is by engaging in critical inquiry and thoughtful reflection that teachers construct the most important aspect of their knowledge: personal knowledge.

2.3 Personal Knowledge

If professional and procedural knowledge systems represent the collective wisdom of the expert, personal knowledge reflects the individual endeavor of the teacher. It is an offshoot of teachers' reflection and reaction, insights and intuition. It signifies their thought processes sedimented through observations, experiences, and interpretations that span a long period before, during, and after formal teacher education programs. Over time, teachers accumulate an unexplained and sometimes unexplainable awareness of what constitutes good teaching. This cumulative awareness has been termed variously as teachers' *sense-making* (van Manen 1977), teachers' *sense of plausibility* (Prabhu 1990), and teachers' *ethic of practicality* (Hargreaves 1994).

Teachers' personal knowledge involves the ability to critically recognize, reflect, review, and reinvent their own identities, beliefs, and values (see Chapter 4 for details). It matures over time as they learn to cope with competing pulls and pressures related to professional preparation, personal beliefs, institutional constraints, learner expectations, assessment instruments, and other factors. Such a critical engagement leads them to "continued recreation of personal meaning" (Diamond 1993: 56) that helps them

> see themselves as capable of imagining and trying alternatives – and eventually as self-directing and self-determining.
>
> *(Ibid.: 52)*

The continued recreation of personal meaning is a long and lonely journey. Not everybody follows the same route, not everybody reaches the same destination. Neither the path nor the process is clear. One reason is that teachers' personal knowledge is considered to be implicit knowledge (or, in Polanyi's term, tacit knowledge) that defies experimental verification or explicit articulation. It has been suggested that teachers pursue their personal knowledge mainly through problem-solving and practical reasoning (Woods 1996, Bartels 2006). When teachers encounter problems in classroom teaching, they usually try to solve them by paying close attention to clues and signs emanating from observable student behavior and from measurable learning outcomes, and by inferring the impact of their action in light of their professional knowledge as well as their personal experience. Such a view is consistent with what cognitive psychologists say about the nature of implicit knowledge (Bereiter & Scardamalia 1993).

Teachers' personal knowledge is the least understood form of teacher knowledge. What is clear though is that it is very much linked to the particular, the practical, and the possible (see section 1.2 in Chapter 1). As has been rightly pointed out (Elbaz 1983: 5), it encompasses the teacher's first hand experience of students' learning styles, interests, needs, strengths and difficulties, and a repertoire of instructional techniques and classroom management skills. The teacher knows the social structure of the school and what it requires, of teacher and student, for survival and for success; she knows the community of which the school is a part, and has a sense of what it will and will not accept.

Personal knowledge is thus acutely responsive to the particularities of local social, cultural, and educational factors that determine learning and teaching in a specific context. And as such, it can come only out of direct participation in classroom processes and events.

As Jean Clandinin (1992) points out, teachers construct and reconstruct their personal knowledge as they live out their stories and retell and relive them through a continual process of self-reflection. Ultimately, it is this personal knowledge that guides them in the practice of everyday teaching. And yet, personal knowledge is rather idiosyncratic in nature, as it varies from teacher to teacher, from context to context. In addition, it

> can be strongly influenced by intuitions, myths, and folk theories, which at times coincide with well-informed views and which at others fly in the face of axiomatic principles widely held among LT professionals.
>
> *(Hedgcock 2002: 302)*

Because of the idiosyncratic nature of teachers' personal knowledge, many researchers do not value it as much as they value academic theories that constitute the professional knowledge base. Without overtly dismissing the importance of personal knowledge, they point out that "there are serious epistemological problems in identifying as knowledge that which teachers believe, imagine, intuit, sense, and reflect upon. It is not that such mental activities may not lead to knowledge; rather, it is that these mental events, once inferred or expressed, must be subjected to assessment for their epistemic merit" (Fenstermacher 1994: 47). Assessing the "epistemic merit" of teacher knowledge remains an intractable challenge largely because it is easy to identify a body of knowledge, but difficult to identify ways of knowing.

Identifying and understanding teachers' ways of knowing and the connection between what they know and what they do has been the focus of research on teacher cognition. Borrowing theoretical concepts from cognitive psychology, researchers in the field of teacher cognition try to study how teachers acquire professional and personal knowledge, how they store it in the mental repertoire, and how they retrieve and use it on demand. In a seminal study on L2 teacher cognition, Devon Woods (1996) has proposed interrelated propositions of BAK (beliefs, assumptions, knowledge) which "do not refer to distinct concepts, but rather to points on a spectrum of meaning" (p. 197). According to him, BAK shapes teachers' interpretations of various types of teaching events: (i) classroom events (including such structures as exchanges and utterances in the classroom), (ii) the curriculum (including higher level teaching structures, such institutionally-imposed organizational units of a course), (iii) textbook approaches, (iv) texts from the theoretical and research literature, (v) pedagogical concepts, and (vi) approaches to planning.

(Ibid.: 213)

But, how exactly teachers use BAK in their decision-making process still remains an open question.

A more recent attempt at explaining teachers' ways of knowing hypothesizes that teachers, stimulated by their close encounters in the classroom, create on-the-spot explanations or courses of action based on their personal knowledge gained through experience and feedback from engaging in teaching, and through deliberate, thoughtful practice (Bartels 2006). Here again, how teachers create on-the-spot courses of action is not fully understood. As Fenstermacher (1994: 54) rightly observes,

the challenge for teacher knowledge research is not simply one of showing us that teachers think, believe, or have opinions but that they know. And, even more important, that they know that they know.

Because of the complex nature of teachers' ways of knowing and the difficulty involved in studying them, we still are quite uncertain about them.

2.4 In Closing

In this chapter, I focused on teacher knowledge which has been researched extensively in the field of general education, and to some extent, in applied linguistics. Questioning the pedagogic value of the bewildering array of labels and definitions for teacher knowledge one finds in the literature, I opted for a simpler frame of reference: professional knowledge, procedural knowledge, and personal knowledge. The first pertains to the intellectual content of a discipline produced and disseminated by experts, the second to the instructional management strategies needed to create and sustain a classroom environment in which desired learning outcomes are made possible, and the third to the individual teacher's sense of plausibility, a sense of what works and what doesn't.

In outlining various aspects of teachers' professional, procedural and personal knowledge, I actually started the chapter highlighting a philosophical distinction between knowledge and knowing. Knowledge as a product, though important, is less valued and valuable than knowing as a process. But, we know very little about teachers' ways of knowing because the cognitive dimension of knowing is so complex and so difficult to investigate. Until we know, with confidence, what teachers think and know, and how they know what they know, our knowledge of teacher knowledge will remain partial and puzzling.

Rapid Reader Response

Write a quick response to the following questions. Form small groups, share your thoughts and discuss them with other members of the group.

1 What is the one big point you learned from this chapter?
2 What is the one main unanswered question you leave the chapter with?
3 What is the one surprising idea or concept you encountered in this chapter?
4 What is the one example of terminology or concept you do not fully understand?

Reflective Tasks

Task 2.1 The Professional

T2.1.1 Presented in this chapter are three types of knowledge: professional, procedural and personal. They are closely connected and they interact with each other. Based on your teaching experience and/or your "apprenticeship of observation" during your student days, think and talk about how a teacher's practice of everyday teaching is actually the result of a concoction of the three types of knowledge brewed by the teacher him/herself.

T2.1.2 Take any one specific feature of professional knowledge (it doesn't matter whether your choice is from the segment on language, language learning or language teaching) and discuss how its classroom manifestation (i.e., how it is implemented by the teacher) might reveal traces of a professional, procedural, and personal knowledge base.

T2.1.3 Professional knowledge has been described as something that experts produce. Under what circumstances do (or can) teachers produce professional knowledge? When does (or can) teachers' personal knowledge get recognized as professional knowledge? If teacher knowing is more important than expert knowledge, why do you think experts' professional knowledge has been privileged over teachers' personal knowledge?

Task 2.2 The Personal

T2.2.1 Personal knowledge signifies the teacher's "thought processes sedimented through observations, experiences, and interpretations that span a long period before, during and after formal teacher education programs." Focusing on any one period (before, during, or after) and selecting any one specific example, discuss how a particular feature of your personal knowledge is dependent on or free from the influence of the formal teacher education program that you are familiar with.

T2.2.2 "Over time, teachers accumulate an unexplained and sometimes unexplainable awareness of what constitutes good teaching." Why is it unexplained? Why is it unexplainable? If it is unexplained and unexplainable, how do (or can) teachers articulate the rationale, and justify the decision, governing their teaching acts?

T2.2.3 Teachers' personal knowledge is deeply connected to the operating principles of particularity, practicality and possibility. Recall the characteristics of these principles from section 1.2 in Chapter 1. Think and talk about what kind of an impact each of the principles can potentially have in shaping teachers' personal knowledge.

Exploratory Project

Project 2.1 The Procedural

The objective of this project is to help you explore and understand the classroom management strategies that facilitate the achievement of desired learning outcomes.

P2.1.1 Think about the best teacher you ever had. How would you describe the "classroom culture" that prevailed? What, do you think, made that possible?

P2.1.2 If you have an intensive English language institute on or near your campus, observe one or two sessions of an ESL class. (Or, observe any foreign language class.) If the class teacher permits, video/audiotape the sessions; if not, take detailed notes.

P2.1.3 Do a "quick and dirty" classroom discourse analysis focusing specifically on classroom management strategies. Focus on issues such as (a) talk structure; (b) question types; (c) student initiation of topics; (d) wait time; and (e) any other.

P2.1.4 Talk to the teacher after your analysis. Get his/her perspectives on the classroom culture that he/she has created. What role did the students play in creating and sustaining the classroom culture? Compare and contrast your perspective with his/hers.

P2.1.5 It is generally believed that teacher education programs do not explicitly focus on helping prospective teachers develop their procedural knowledge. How does the teacher education program you are associated with incorporate classroom management strategies in its curriculum? Or, does it?

3

ANALYZING

To be self-determined is to endorse one's actions at the highest level of reflection. When one is self-determined, people experience a sense of freedom to do what is interesting, personally important, and vitalizing.

(Edward Deci & Richard Ryan 2008)

3.0 Introduction

This module—analyzing—is based on the assumption that in order to carry out their duties responsibly and successfully, L2 teachers must develop the knowledge and skill necessary to analyze and understand learner needs, learner motivation, and learner autonomy. What makes such an analysis and understanding so complicated and challenging is that learner needs, motivation, and autonomy are determined by a combination of individual, institutional, governmental, and societal demands. These demands, sometimes competing with each other, change from context to context and from time to time. The emerging global society and the economic opportunities it brings with it are changing English language policy and planning in a number of countries. For instance, English was taught in India for a long time as "a library language" focusing on reading comprehension so that learners could read and understand books and journals in English, mainly for purposes of research and development in science and technology. Now, the emphasis is gradually shifting to the development of communicative abilities in learners so that they can fully exploit the unlimited possibilities that the globalized job market has opened up. One sees similar reorientation of English language policy and planning in countries as far away as Brazil and Colombia in South America, and Japan and South Korea in Southeast Asia.

A systematic analysis of learner needs, motivation, and autonomy addresses macro-level socio-economic and educational factors as well as micro-level matters related to learners' language use and learning purposes, such as: in what situations learners will be using the target language; why are they enrolling in a language program; and what kind of learning strategies and styles they bring with them, etc. Such a detailed analysis is traditionally carried out by language planners, syllabus designers, or text-book writers. However, teachers have to be aware of it in order to gear their classroom activities to meet the needs, motivation, and autonomy of any given group of learners. In addition, they may have to reassess and recast the analysis done by outsiders by taking into account the particularity of their learning and teaching situations.

In the following sections, I briefly discuss learner needs, motivation, and autonomy relating them to each other. It will become clear that the growing demands and expectations of a global society are changing the nature of learner needs, motivation, and autonomy thereby exposing the inadequacy of traditional ways of analyzing and understanding them.

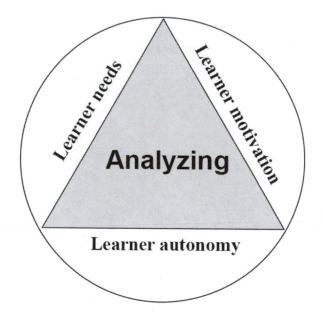

3.1 Learner Needs

A simple definition of learner needs states that it is the gap between what is and what should be (Brindley 1984). The central aim of a needs analysis, therefore, is to discover what language learners have to learn, what they like to learn, and what they have not yet learned, corresponding roughly to learner needs, wants, and lacks. Learner needs are generally determined not by learners themselves but by other stakeholders, such as policy makers, teachers, institutions, education ministries, and employers. Because learners may perceive their needs differently, teachers may have to address what Brindley (1984) has called *objective* needs and *subjective* needs. Teachers can diagnose the objective needs of their learners on the basis of needs analysis already done by outsiders and also on the basis of personal data about a given group of learners that they themselves can collect in their classroom. Subjective needs are likes, dislikes, wants, and expectations of learners and can be diagnosed only with their willing cooperation, and active participation.

The importance of analyzing learner wants (or subjective needs) can hardly be overstated because, "a need does not exist independent of a person" (Richterich 1984: 29). By doing a "wants" analysis, teachers can identify particular expectations of a given group of learners and try to address them in their classes. Teachers can do a "wants" analysis by administering specially prepared survey questionnaires that focus on learner perception of learning purpose as well as on their learning styles and strategies. In fact, the results of such survey questionnaires can be used as a teaching item thereby facilitating negotiated interaction in class.

Wants as perceived by learners may at times come into conflict with the needs assessment done by analysts including teachers. Any failure to be sensitive to learner wants may lead to failure in creating and sustaining learner motivation. This kind of mismatch can also shape learners' classroom behavior, particularly in terms of the value placed on classroom activities, the attention given, and the effort made (Nunan 1989). Such a scenario seems to be playing out in some Asian countries, where a vast number of learners from poorly-staffed, badly-equipped government–run schools flock to private language centers that have mushroomed in major cities so that they can gain much needed English communicative abilities.

Closely related to needs and wants are lacks. The target proficiency "needs to be matched against the existing proficiency of the learners. The gap between the two can be referred to as the learner's lacks" (Hutchinson & Waters 1987: 56). A targeted diagnostic test will easily reveal what the learners' lack in terms of such linguistic features as grammatical constructions, sentence types, clauses, vocabulary, speech acts, etc. However, a focus on language-oriented lacks will result only in a limited understanding of lacks. Teachers should also be aware of individual, social, cultural, economic, institutional, and logistical factors that constrain classroom activities and events. Lack of essential resources such as textbooks, audio-visual aids, etc., should also be the focus of such an analysis of lacks.

There are several ways in which relevant data can be collected for analyzing learner needs, wants, and lacks. They include survey questionnaires, personal interviews, placement tests, classroom observation, and self-report. It is advisable to ensure triangulation in conducting needs analysis. That is, the analyst must gather a variety of perspectives on what language learners in a particular context need to learn. These perspectives may come from various players including learners, teachers, parents, administrators, and others. Each of these players will have a different idea of what exactly the language learners should focus on for improving their second language skills. Such a wide range of perspectives is crucial because they feed directly into the designing of the syllabus for a course. They determine the general goals, specific objectives, and curricular content of a course, ensuring its relevance.

Related to the issue of triangulation is the role of the analyst as an insider or an outsider to a particular language learning and teaching community. An insider (a practicing teacher, for instance) may have a better idea about the linguistic needs of her students. However, an outsider trained in the identification of necessary communicative acts may have a better idea of the specific areas where communicative skills need to be improved. A useful illustration comes from the Indian Institute of Science (Ramani et al. 1988). The Indian researchers were conducting a needs analysis in order to design a need-based, English language course for students specializing in industrial design. An interview with scientists at the Institute revealed that a mandatory seminar in design was meant to be a chance for the students to defend their design choices and not simply to provide progress reports on their designs. This distinction between argumentation and reporting would have gone unnoticed by the analysts if its importance had not been stressed by their colleagues in other departments. Made aware of the outsider-perspective, the analysts were able to make appropriate curricular changes in their English course in order to meet the specific needs of their students.

The importance given to needs analysis can be traced back to the development of the communicative approach to language teaching during the late '70s and early '80s. The approach emphasized the centrality of language needs of the learner, leading to the designing of need-based, learner-centered curriculum for teaching English for general as well as for specific purposes. During this period, needs analysis largely meant analyzing language skills necessary for learners to communicate effectively in either a general or a specific (i.e., mostly job-related) setting. This narrow interpretation, dubbed as the product-oriented view, was criticized for its limitations, and was contrasted with a broader process-oriented view focused on the needs of the learner as an individual (Brindley 1984). The broader perspective takes into account the affective and cognitive variables that influence learning because it was felt that learners' needs are intertwined with other attributes such as motivation, cognitive development, learning styles and strategies, attitudes, and beliefs. It was deemed necessary to look at these factors because of the impact they may have on learner success.

Focusing on the limitations of even the broader version of needs analysis, Sarah Benesch (2001: 61) points out that needs has been wrongly treated as

> a psychological term suggesting that students require or want what the institution mandates. It conflates the private world of desire with the public world of requirements, rules and regulations. It implies that students will be fulfilled if they follow the rules.

Benesch demonstrates how needs analysis overlooks the distinction between institutional demands and individual needs, and how it hides power struggles that are embedded in educational decision-making. In short, the political and ideological nature of needs analysis has long been ignored. To address these drawbacks, Benesch (Ibid.: 43) proposes *critical needs analysis,* which includes an examination of

> who sets the goals, why they were formulated, whose interests are served by them, and whether they should be challenged.

By incorporating learner needs and learner rights, the critical alternative seeks to help learners

> articulate and formalize their resistance, to participate more democratically as members of an academic community and in the larger society.
>
> *(Ibid.: 43)*

The critical alternative with its emphasis on learner needs and learner rights has the potential to pave the way for greater learner participation in classroom activities leading to increased and sustainable learner motivation.

3.2 Learner Motivation

"*Given motivation,*" declared Pit Corder forty-five years ago, "it is inevitable that a human being will learn a second language if he is exposed to the language data" (1967: 164, original emphasis). True to his observation, learner motivation has been consistently found to be one crucial variable that correlates well with successful L2 development. Most studies on L2 motivation have been inspired by the distinction Canadian social psychologists Robert Gardner and Wallace Lambert (1972) made between integrative motivation and instrumental motivation. The former refers to an interest in learning an L2 in order to culturally integrate with members of the target language community while the latter refers to an interest in learning an L2 for functional purposes, such as getting a job or passing an examination. In their early studies, Gardner and his colleagues (see Gardner 1985 for a consolidated review of the literature) reported that integrative motivation is far superior to instrumental motivation. However, studies conducted in other learning and teaching contexts failed to show its superiority (Lukmani 1972, Chihara & Oller 1978). In fact, a comprehensive review of motivational studies found a wide range of correlations covering all possibilities: positive, nil, negative, and ambiguous (Au 1988). In their subsequent investigations, Gardner and his colleagues themselves found that both integrative motivation and instrumental motivation have "consistent and meaningful effects on learning and on behavioral indices of learning" (Gardner & MacIntyre 1991: 69). In spite of the research findings that are clearly ambiguous, the concept of integrative motivation has for a long time maintained its alluring appeal.

An important aspect of integrative motivation that has generated considerable debate is its basic premise that L2 learners must show "a sincere and personal interest in the people and culture represented by the other group" (Gardner & Lambert

1972: 132) and that they "must be willing to identify with members of another ethnolinguistic group and take on very subtle aspects of their behaviour" (Ibid.: 135). There are several factors that weaken such an argument.

At its broadest level, social psychologists' invocation of social identification and ethnolinguistic affiliation as motives for and markers of successful L2 development betray an unwelcome, perhaps unintended, association with the nativist assumption that cultural assimilation should be the ultimate goal for immigrants as well as for L2 learners. Proponents of such a view saw integrative motivation as the preferred path to the desired destination of cultural assimilation (see Kumaravadivelu 2008 for details). The invocation is also reminiscent of the strong version of the discredited Whorfian hypothesis which claimed that languages and cultures are inextricably linked. Postcolonial writers such as Salman Rushdie, Chinua Achebe, and others have shown how a Western language can be profitably reconstructed into a vehicle for expressing sociocultural nuances that are completely alien to the Western culture, thereby proving that languages and cultures are not inextricably linked (Kumaravadivelu 2003a).

A closely related factor is the emergence of world Englishes with their amazing form, function, and spread. Postcolonial societies in Asia and Africa that have adopted English as an additional language quickly recognized that English is indisputably linked to the cultural imperialism associated with colonialism, and that it comes with heavy cultural baggage. One of the ways in which they tried to decolonize English is through the process of nativization (Kachru 1983), a process of indigenizing the phonological, syntactic, pragmatic, and cultural aspects of the English language. A central goal was to erase the lingering traces of English imperialism and to claim ownership of the English language, along with its learning and teaching enterprise. Whether this goal has been achieved or not is an open question.

The issue of the ownership of English triggered by the growth of world Englishes has rekindled the debate about the relevance of integrative motivation for L2 development. Following a categorical assertion that "the notion of integrativeness is untenable for second-language learners in world Englishes contexts" (Coetzee-Van Rooy, 2006: 447), researchers in L2 motivation (Ushioda & Dörnyei 2009: 2–3) have begun to

> ask whether we can apply the concept of integrative motivation when there is no specific target reference group of speakers. Does it make sense to talk about integrative motivation when ownership of English does not necessarily rest with a specific community of speakers, whether native speakers of British or American English varieties or speakers of World English varieties?

An even more consequential development that has a direct bearing on the relevance of integrative motivation is the on-going process of globalization and its unfailing impact on language education in general and on identity formation in particular (see Kumaravadivelu 2008 for details). As briefly discussed in Chapter 1, globalization, particularly cultural globalization, has presented most of the people around the world with unparalleled opportunities for cultural growth, and unparalleled threats to their national and cultural identity. As a result, people everywhere are becoming more and more conscious of the need to learn English and also of the need to preserve and protect their national linguistic and cultural identities. They realize that in choosing and forming identities in this globalized world, they require critical knowledge that can help them tell the difference between information and disinformation, and between ideas and ideologies. The Internatization of information systems makes such critical knowledge available to those individuals who seek it. Using the easily accessible knowledge-base and engaging in critical self-reflection, individuals now have the opportunity to evaluate their and others' cultural value systems and develop a global cultural consciousness that has the potential to enrich their lives (Kumaravadivelu 2008).

Given the expanding global cultural consciousness, it is rather naïve to continue to believe that L2 learners would be integratively motivated. Egged on by national and regional forces which make sure that the local linguistic and cultural identities are not sacrificed at the altar of cultural globalization, language policy planners around the world are trying to design the teaching of English as a tool for international, and in some cases intra-national, communication, and as a resource for tapping the global job market. The fact that the non-English speaking world learns and uses English language for communicational purposes and not for cultural identity formation is becoming increasingly clear. Indian scholars tell us that Indians learn English to meet their educational and institutional needs and they keep it separate from their cultural beliefs and practices (Krishnaswamy & Burde 1998). Similarly, Indonesian learners of English are driven by their vision of an English-speaking, globally-involved citizenship that is firmly rooted in the local or national identity as Indonesians (Lamb 2004). For Pakistanis, English reflects Islamic values, and embodies South Asian Islamic sensitivities (Mahboob 2009). The Turks have no difficulty whatsoever in privileging "their Turkish and Muslim identities over the Western way of existence presented during English-language courses" (Atay & Ece 2009: 31). Contributors to the volumes edited by Kubota & Lin (2009) and Lin (2008) confirm how most learners of English across the world see it and use it as a communicational tool.

The increased awareness of the impact of cultural globalization and the perceived need to preserve local linguistic and cultural identities have not escaped the attention of L2 motivation researchers. Emphasizing the importance of integrating theories of identity with theories of second language acquisition, Bonny Norton has proposed the motivational concept of *investment* which "conceives of the language learner as having a complex social history and multiple desires" (Norton 2000: 10). She rightly points out that

> an investment in the target language is also an investment in a learner's own identity, an identity which is constantly changing across time and space.
>
> *(Ibid.: 11)*

Furthermore, as Kumaravadivelu (2002: 49) points out, there is also a realization that

> because of greater contacts between people of different cultures, and because of awareness of each other's values and visions, any attempt to use the globalized English language as an instrument of cultural imperialism is bound to fail.

Consequently, several scholars now see and seek a "paradigmatic shift" in the L2 motivation research agenda. According to some of them, L2 motivation

> is currently in the process of being radically reconceptualised and retheorised in the context of contemporary notions of self and identity.
>
> *(Ushioda & Dörnyei 2009: 1)*

Contemporary notions of Self and identity are largely drawn from postmodernism, which sees individual identity as multiple and dynamic (see Chapter 4, section 4.1. for more details). Drawing from the postmodern thoughts on Self, identity and agency, and applying them to L2 motivation research, Dörnyei (2009) has proposed what he has called "L2 Motivational Self System." The system is made up of three components: (1) the ideal L2 Self, a representation of the attributes that one would ideally like to possess (i.e., representation of hopes, aspirations, or wishes); (2) the ought-to self, a representation of attributes that one believes one ought to possess (i.e., meeting expectations and avoiding possible negative outcomes); and (3) L2 learning experience, a representation of motives related to the immediate learning environment and experience (i.e., the impact of the teacher, the curriculum, the peer group, and experience of success). The three components of the Motivational Self System offer new avenues for analyzing and understanding L2 motivation. Supporting this possibility is a qualitative analysis of L2 identity and L2 motivation among English L1 speakers of French in the French Foreign Legion. The analysis suggests that

> motivation is context-dependent, multifaceted and dynamic, and that changes in individuals' motivation to learn L2 are better explained by reference to ongoing processes of identification, differentiation and the L2 learning experience.
>
> *(Lyons 2009: 249)*

In addition to postmodern thoughts, developments in cognitive psychology are providing valuable conceptual resources for the study of L2 motivation and identity. Self-Determination Theory (SDT) is one of them. Introduced by Edward Deci & Richard Ryan (1985), SDT is an elaboration of the well-established cognitive psychological theory of intrinsic and extrinsic motivation. Intrinsic motivation is the desire to engage in activities characterized by enjoyment. There is no apparent reward except the experience of enjoying the activity itself. Individuals seek out and engage in intrinsically motivated activities in order to feel competent and self-determining. Like basic human drives, intrinsic needs are innate to the human organism and function as an important energizer of behavior. Extrinsic motivation can be triggered only by external cues, which include gaining and maintaining approval, or avoiding disapproval, and gaining or losing specific tangible rewards. It is conditioned by the practical considerations of life with all its attendant sense of struggle, success, or failure. Thus, extrinsic motivation is associated with lower levels of self-esteem and higher levels of anxiety, compared to intrinsic motivation.

The Self-Determination Theory, derived from empirical studies, postulates that human beings have three core psychological needs: competence (i.e., one's belief in the ability to influence and accomplish desired outcomes), relatedness (i.e., one's need to have satisfying and supportive social relationships), and autonomy (i.e., one's experience of acting with a sense of choice, volition, and self-determination). These core needs are seen to be stimulated and sustained by a combination of intrinsic motivation and certain types of extrinsic motivation, with the former playing a crucial and deciding role. The importance given to intrinsic motivation in SDT echoes the postmodern concept of Self because, as Deci and Ryan (2000: 231) point out, intrinsic motivation entails volition—"the organismic desire to self-organize experience and behavior and to have activity be concordant with one's integrated sense of self." By linking volition, self-organizing experience and self-determination together, SDT theorists make the vital point that motivation is deeply linked to autonomy.

3.3 Learner Autonomy

Autonomy, according to SDT theorists (Deci & Ryan 2000: 235), is not only a universal human characteristic but it is also an extension of a deeply evolved tendency in animate life, describing as it does the propensities toward self-regulation of action and coherence in the organism's behavioral aims. And, as such, the human need for autonomy, along with the needs for competence and relatedness, transcend cultures and contexts. In a recent cross-cultural study on autonomy, Valeryi Chirkov (2009: 254) dispels the widespread "conceptual confusion" that

> inhabitants of Eastern nations are so strongly collectivistic that it is in their nature to avoid autonomy and personal freedom

and declares that cultures

> differentially designate domains in which members of the society may exercise this fundamental need, and shape the appropriate activities through which autonomous motivation can be practiced.

In other words, different cultures assign different meanings and interpretations to the idea of autonomy, and provide different forms of support to cultivate the spirit of autonomy.

Like their colleagues in cognitive psychology and general education, L2 researchers have emphasized the importance of autonomy in language learning and teaching. In a state-of-the-art article, Phil Benson (2006) traces the growth of interest in autonomy among L2 researchers and teachers starting with the Council of Europe's Modern Languages Project in the early 1980s. The project defined learner autonomy as "the ability to take charge of one's own learning" (Holec 1981: 3). Others expanded this definition to include the development and exercise of a capacity for critical reflection, decision making, and independent action on the part of the learner (Little 1991: 4). Thus, truly autonomous learners are expected to assume responsibility for determining the goals and objectives, the content and method of their learning, as well as for monitoring its progress and evaluating its outcomes. Later, doubting whether such a total autonomy was realistic for most L2 learners, William Littlewood (1999) made a distinction between proactive and reactive autonomy. In the former, learners themselves set up, at least partially, their own directions for learning. In the latter, learners organize their resources autonomously in order to reach their goal once a direction has been set up for them.

There seems to be a symbiotic relationship between learner autonomy and learning strategies. In a recent review of research, Rebecca Oxford (2011) identified learner autonomy as one of the recurring themes in the literature on learning strategies. The connection is not hard to see because learning strategies, after all, deal with learners' goal-oriented actions directed towards achieving language development, and learner autonomy is a crucial part of that effort. It is, therefore, not surprising that early work on learner autonomy in L2 learning and teaching was largely concerned with language learning strategies and with training learners in using them success- fully. Researchers provided useful taxonomies of learning strategies that described learners' cognitive, metacognitive, affective, social, and compensation strategies, and also provided step by step strategy instruction (O'Malley & Chamot 1990; Oxford 1990). Subsequent research revealed that good language learners use a range of strategies for different language skill areas and purposes, depending on factors such as age, motivation, culture, and nationality (see Griffiths, ed. 2008 for details). The overall purpose has been to make learners more active participants in their language learning, and to make teachers more sensitive to learner autonomy and learning difficulties. Undoubtedly, the wealth of information now available on learning strategies and learner training opens up opportunities for learners to exercise their autonomy and maximize their learning potential.

Characterizing the strategy-based learner autonomy as necessary but not sufficient, some scholars (Benson 1997, Pennycook 1997) have sought to expand the notion of learner autonomy in order to embrace

> issues such as the societal context in which learning takes place, roles and relationships in the classroom and outside, kinds of learning tasks, and the content of the language that is learned.
>
> *(Benson 1997: 32)*

Becoming an autonomous language learner and user is considered

> not so much a question of learning how to learn as it is a question of learning
> how to struggle for cultural alternatives.
>
> *(Pennycook 1997: 45)*

The addition of sociocultural and political dimensions to learner autonomy follows the tenets of critical pedagogy advocated by Paulo Freire (1972) and focuses on the transformative role that learners and teachers are expected to play (see Chapter 1).

In this context, Kumaravadivelu (2003b) has made a distinction between narrow and broad approaches to learner autonomy. The narrow approach maintains that the goal of learner autonomy is to learn to learn while the broad approach maintains that the goal should be to learn to liberate. The narrow view involves enabling learners to learn how to learn by equipping them with the tools necessary to learn on their own, and training them to use appropriate strategies for realizing their learning objectives. The primary focus "is on the learner's academic achievement through strategic engagement" (Kumaravadivelu 2003b: 133).

Unlike the narrow approach that treats learning to learn as an end in itself, the broad approach treats learning to learn only as a means to an end, the end being learning to liberate. The former stands for academic autonomy and the latter, liberatory autonomy. Thus, as Kumaravadivelu (2003b: 141) observes:

> while academic autonomy enables learners to be strategic practitioners in
> order to realize their learning potential, liberatory autonomy empowers them
> to be critical thinkers in order to realize their human potential.

Following the tenets of critical pedagogy, liberatory autonomy actively seeks to help learners recognize sociopolitical impediments placed on their paths to progress, and to provide them with the intellectual tools necessary to overcome them. What the learning-to-liberate approach emphasizes is that if we are seriously committed to helping learners become autonomous individuals, then, we need to take into account the sociopolitical factors that shape the culture of the L2 classroom.

A clear connection between liberatory autonomy and motivation has recently been drawn by L2 motivation researchers. Combining Vygotskian sociocultural theory and Freirean critical pedagogy, Ema Ushioda (2006: 149) argues that both autonomy and motivation have "an inescapably political dimension of which we need to take much greater account in our research and pedagogical practice." She suggests that any critical perspective on the socially constructed process of the motivation to learn a second language must be framed within a theory of autonomy. This entails, according to her, the need for L2 learners/users to develop critical awareness of the cultural constructions, ideologies, and social positioning in the discourses to which they are exposed in order for them to effectively exercise their agency and develop their own voice. The politics of motivation, Ushioda argues (2006: 158):

relate not simply to questions of language choice but also to the day-to-day processes of engagement with language learning, language use and social context.

Some of these developments in L2 motivation and autonomy are turning out to be responsive to the demands of the on-going process of globalization as well. Several leading universities, particularly from the UK, the USA, Europe, and Australia are aggressively recruiting foreign students and some of them are actively setting up outposts overseas. Consequently, educational policies and practices are getting more and more globalized. Along with them, an emphasis on autonomy and individuality is fast becoming a global trend in educational circles. It has been rightly pointed out that the spread of communicative and task-based approaches to language teaching and the use of self-access and computer-assisted instructional strategies and materials have favored practices associated with autonomy in language learning (Benson 2006). The expansion of the scope of autonomy to include individual and social constructs such as self-determination, self-motivation, agency, and identity has been a helpful development that is sensitive to the demands of a globalized society.

3.4 Classroom Implications

The new developments in the areas of learner needs, motivation, and autonomy discussed above present both opportunities and challenges for teachers and teacher educators. Several studies conducted in the field of general education that were grounded in Self-Determination Theory show that

> teachers' support of students' basic psychological needs for autonomy, competence, and relatedness facilitates students' autonomous self-regulation for learning, academic performance, and wellbeing.
>
> *(Niemiec & Ryan 2009: 133)*

Important conclusions that have been drawn from the studies include: (a) classroom activities and tasks that are supportive of autonomy are conducive to students' intrinsic motivation; (b) students learn better and are more creative when intrinsically motivated; and (c) teachers can either allow intrinsic motivation to flourish and deeper learning to occur, or thwart those processes depending on whether they succeed in designing and using learning tasks that contribute to students' satisfaction of the basic psychological needs for competence, autonomy and relatedness (Niemiec & Ryan 2009). We are also reminded

> that teachers can achieve these goals by "providing choice and meaningful rationales for learning activities, acknowledging students' feelings about those topics, and minimizing pressure and control.
>
> *(Ibid.: 140)*

In addition, educationists advise teachers to develop "a deeply rooted willingness and capacity to take and prioritize the students' perspective during learning activities," and to ask self-reflective questions such as:

> "If I were the student (rather than the teacher), what would I want the teacher to do?", and "Is the subject matter important and useful to my students and, if so, how can I highlight that personal relevance?"
>
> *(Reeve & Halusic 2009: 146)*

In the field of L2 learning and teaching, David Little (2009) has proposed three basic principles that might contribute to the promotion of learner motivation and autonomy. The principle of learner involvement requires that teachers involve learners fully in planning, monitoring, and evaluating their own learning. The principle of learner reflection requires that teachers help learners to reflect continuously on the process and content of their learning and to engage in regular self-assessment. The principle of target language use requires that teachers ensure that the target language is the medium as well as the goal of learning, including its reflective component. These three principles

> describe at a very general level the things teachers have to do to create and sustain an autonomous language learning community.
>
> *(Ibid.: 224)*

At a higher level of promoting meaningful liberatory autonomy in the language classroom, teachers have to follow strategies such as (a) encouraging learners to assume the role of mini-ethnographers so that they can investigate and understand how language use is socially structured and ideologically loaded; (b) helping them write diaries or journal entries about issues that directly engage their sense of who they are and how they relate to the world they live in; (c) enabling them to think critically and develop interpretive capabilities needed to contest the regulated representations of language and culture normally found in prescribed textbooks; and (d) providing opportunities for them to explore the unfolding frontiers in cyberspace and the unlimited possibilities offered by the Internatization of communication, and bringing back to the class their own topics for discussion and their own perspectives on those topics (Kumaravadivelu 2003b: 142–43). Taken together, these and other similar strategies will help learners develop an overall academic ability, intellectual competence, social consciousness, and mental attitude necessary to avail opportunities and overcome challenges presented by a globalized society.

Clearly, our globalized society is demanding new ways of analyzing and under-standing learner needs, learner motivation, and learner autonomy, and their complex interactions. Given these demands, the challenges faced by prospective and practi-cing teachers can be daunting. Expert analysts who put together a language program will do some preliminary work of analyzing learner needs, motivation, and autonomy. It will then be up to the teachers to reassess it in light of the particularity of their own learning and teaching contexts. Any advantage accruing from successful curriculum, methods, and materials could quickly be cancelled out if proper analysis of learner needs, motivation, and autonomy is not done. Teachers can minimize their demands on time and effort for doing this kind of analysis if they involve learners themselves as part of this analytical exploration and use the results of such analysis as teaching items.

The challenges faced by prospective and practicing teachers place a heavy burden on teacher educators. It is clear that an important feature of the globalized educational setting

> is the unique capacity invested in the teacher (as an influential member of the classroom social microcosm) to develop her students' critical awareness of the very barriers, constraints and ideologies in the surrounding social context that limit their autonomy and motivation.
>
> *(Ushioda 2006: 159)*

It is the teacher educator who has to play a crucial role in the development of such a unique capacity.

Just as we expect our prospective and practicing teachers to create an autonomous classroom that is sensitive to learners' sense of Self, agency, and identity, it is not unreasonable to expect teacher educators to take cognizance of student teachers' identities, beliefs, and values in constructing their curriculum and in conducting classroom events (see Chapter 4 for details). More often than not, student teachers perceive an unmistakable disjunction between what is emphasized and what is enacted during their teacher education programs. Leni Dam (2007: 2) touched upon this issue not long ago. Referring to the constant advice student teachers get about the need to promote learner autonomy, she says:

> Young teachers who had just left teacher training college and who attended my courses told me that they knew how to do this in theory. However, the teaching they had themselves "received" at the college had had no resemblance whatsoever with the theory. Most of the time, their teachers ran their classes in the traditional teacher fronted and teacher-directed way, i.e. with teacher input followed by questions and class discussions.

One way of remedying the persistent practice of the "teacher fronted and teacher-directed way" is to move away from the transmission model of teacher education that seeks to transmit a pre-selected and predetermined body of knowledge to a transformative perspective that seeks to transform an information-oriented teacher education model into an inquiry-oriented one, with the ultimate goal of producing teachers who are autonomous individuals (see Chapter 1, section 1.1.4). As I have argued elsewhere, teacher educators must take into account the importance of recognizing teachers' voices and visions, the imperatives of developing their critical capabilities, and the prudence of achieving both of these through a dialogic construction of meaning.

(Kumaravadivelu 2003a: 552)

Teacher educators will also be able to move away from their "teacher-fronted and teacher-directed way" if they (a) recognize, and help student teachers recognize, the inequalities built into the current teacher education programs that treat teacher educators as producers of knowledge and practicing teachers as consumers of knowledge; (b) encourage prospective teachers to think critically so that they may relate their personal knowledge to the professional knowledge they are being exposed to, monitor how each shapes and is shaped by the other, assess how the generic professional knowledge could be modified to suit particular pedagogic needs and wants, and ultimately derive their own personal theory of practice; and (c) create conditions for prospective teachers to acquire basic skills in classroom discourse analysis that will help them hypothesize pedagogic principles from their classroom practice and thereby demystify the process of theory construction (Kumaravadivelu 2003a: 553; also see Chapter 5, this volume).

3.5 In Closing

The focus of this module has been learner needs, learner motivation and learner autonomy. I discussed how the needs of L2 learners of English have been shifting to include the development of genuine communicative abilities in them so that they can fully exploit the unlimited possibilities that the globalized job market has opened up. Shifting too are motivational factors. I also maintained that the traditional emphasis on integrative motivation has become hopelessly inadequate because of several factors, including the emergence of world Englishes, the changing ownership of English, the on-going cultural globalization and its impact on individual and national identities, the attempts to preserve and protect local linguistic and cultural identities, and the Internatization of information systems that makes critical knowledge widely available. I pointed out that given the expanding global cultural conscious-ness, it is rather naïve to continue to believe that L2 learners would be integratively motivated.

Seeking a "paradigmatic shift" in the L2 motivation research agenda, L2 researchers turned to recent developments in cognitive psychology, to postmodern thoughts, and to critical pedagogy. Developments in these fields have offered much needed conceptual underpinnings. The cognitive psychological theory of Self-Determination (SDT) with its emphasis on intrinsic motivation has directed our attention to the core psychological needs of competence, relatedness, and autonomy. In the process of articulating the close connection between volition, self-organizing experience and self-determination, SDT theorists emphasized the importance of autonomy as well. We learn we need to take seriously not only academic autonomy that focuses on learning strategies necessary for helping learners learn to learn but also liberatory autonomy that focuses on empowering strategies necessary for helping learners to learn to liberate.

Finally, I touched upon some of the classroom implications of the new developments that present both opportunities and challenges for teachers as well as teacher educators. It is now fairly clear that our globalized society is demanding new ways of analyzing and understanding learner needs, learner motivation, and learner autonomy, and their intricate relationships. While an enhanced focus on learners is clearly warranted, an enriched focus on teachers is also required. I turn to that next.

Rapid Reader Response

Write a quick response to the following questions. Form small groups, share your thoughts and discuss them with other members of the group.

1 What is the one big point you learned from this chapter?
2 What is the one main unanswered question you leave the chapter with?
3 What is the one surprising idea or concept you encountered in this chapter?
4 What is one example of terminology or concept you do not fully understand?

Reflective Tasks

Task 3.1 The Global and the Motivational

T3.1.1 Reproduced here is a statement by Ushioda & Dörnyei (2009). Please read it carefully, form small groups, and discuss the questions that follow. "Put simply, L2 motivation is currently in the process of being radically reconceptualised and retheorised in the context of contemporary notions of self and identity (p. 1) … A basic question we have begun to ask is whether we can apply the concept of integrative motivation when there is no specific target reference group of speakers. Does it make sense to talk about integrative attitudes when ownership of English does not necessarily rest with a specific community of speakers, whether native speakers of British, or American English varieties or speakers of World English varieties?" (p. 2–3).

T3.1.2 Why do you think the concept of integrative motivation has played a prominent role for such a long time in spite of ambiguous research findings?

T3.1.3 Based on your understanding of the contemporary notions of Self and identity, and your knowledge of L2 motivation theories, do you agree (or disagree) that L2 motivation needs to be "radically reconceptualised and retheorised"? What are your reasons?

T3.1.4 Given the process of globalization and the varied purposes for which people around the world learn English, how should we re-examine our understanding of L2 motivation? In other words, what factors should such a new understanding take into account?

T3.1.5 How might moving away from the traditional concept of integrative motivation re-shape the policies and practices of L2 teaching?

Task 3.2 The Local and the Practical

T3.2.1 Consider what Leni Dam (2007) has to say about the constant advice student teachers get about the need to promote learner motivation and learner autonomy in class: "Young teachers who had just left teacher training college and who attended my courses told me that they knew how to do this in theory. However, the teaching they had themselves 'received' at the college had had no resemblance whatsoever with the theory. Most of the time, their teachers ran their classes in the traditional teacher fronted and teacher-directed way, i.e. with teacher input followed by questions and class discussions" (p. 2).

T3.2.2 How would you describe the teaching you have "received" (or are "receiving") as part of your teacher education program? Consider issues such as teacher control, learner autonomy, institutional culture, etc.

T3.2.3 What connection (or disconnection) do you notice between what is actually emphasized and what is normally enacted in your teacher education program?

T3.2.4 If you do see a noticeable connection, what are the classroom events and activities that make that connection possible?

T3.2.5 If you do see a noticeable disconnection, what do you think are the factors that contribute to such disconnect?

T3.2.6 To what extent, in your judgment, was/is the teacher education program you were/are associated with sensitive to your sense of Self, agency and identity? Be specific.

Exploratory Project

Project 3.1 Analyzing Needs, Motivation and Autonomy

The general aim of this preliminary project is to help you analyze and understand learner needs, motivation, and autonomy. It involves (a) identifying a client; (b) collecting data; (c) analyzing learner needs, motivation, and autonomy; and (d) determining general goals and specific learning outcomes. You may want to work with a small group of classmates/colleagues.

P3.1.1 Choose a client. Your target client can be any agency/institution in your area that seeks to help L2 learners pursue their language development at any proficiency level. Possible agencies/institutions include your own institution, local Universities, Colleges, and Language Centers (public or private) offering language enrichment courses.

P3.1.2   Once you identify your client, talk to the person(s) in charge of the language program and seek permission to work with/for the agency/institution. Explain to them what your project goals are and how you might be of assistance in helping them design a new, or improve an existing, curriculum.

P3.1.3   The next step is to collect data. You may use any (or a combination of) data eliciting techniques such as interviews, questionnaires, surveys, etc. Your focus is on learner needs, motivation and the degree of autonomy they seek/get. However, your aim is to get the perspectives of a reasonable number of learners, teachers, and administrators.

P3.1.4   Analyze the data. If you need help in framing the questions or analyzing the data, consult any recent book on curriculum design, most of which will have a chapter on needs analysis (for a new volume, see Nation & Macalister, 2010, *Language Curriculum Design*, New York: Routledge).

P3.1.5   Based on your analysis, formulate a set of general goals and specific learning outcomes of a possible short-term course for the student population served by your client agency/institution. State the goals/outcomes in behavioral terms.

P3.1.6   Finally, write a detailed report of your project, suggesting to your client possible ways in which the findings of your analysis can be incorporated in a new (or an existing) curriculum.

4

RECOGNIZING

We teach who we are. … Viewed from this angle, teaching holds a mirror to the soul. If I am willing to look in that mirror and not run from what I see, I have a chance to gain self knowledge – and knowing myself is as crucial to good teaching as knowing my students and my subject.

(Parker J. Palmer 1998: 2)

4.0 Introduction

This module, recognizing, is based on a simple proposition that we cannot separate the teacher from teaching any more than we can separate the dancer from dancing. We learned in the previous two chapters that teachers' professional, personal, and procedural knowledge, and their awareness of learners' needs, motivation, and autonomy are bound to play a crucial role in their success as classroom practitioners. It may, however, be argued that an effective use of such knowledge and awareness depends to a large extent on the teaching Self, that is, the inner Self that teachers bring with them to the practice of everyday teaching. Equally important are their ability and willingness to recognize and renew their teaching Self. It then follows that teacher education programs have a responsibility to encourage and enable present and prospective teachers to reflect seriously on how they construct and reconstruct their teaching Self.

Recognizing the teaching Self is all about recognizing teacher identities, beliefs, and values. That is to say, a teacher's personal disposition toward various aspects of their professional life is so vital that it determines their teaching behavior and hence shapes learning outcome. It contributes to their understanding of and perceptions about what constitutes desired learning and what constitutes desired teaching. It steers them towards either being passive technicians who merely play the role of conduits transmitting a body of knowledge from one source to another or becoming transformative intellectuals who play the role of change agents raising educational, social, cultural, and political consciousness in their learners. It guides their decision-making on a variety of strategies ranging from the simple use of pair or group work in classrooms to the complex task of maximizing learning potential. To understand the teaching Self, it is important that we understand some of its constituent elements, particularly teacher identities, teacher beliefs, and teacher values.

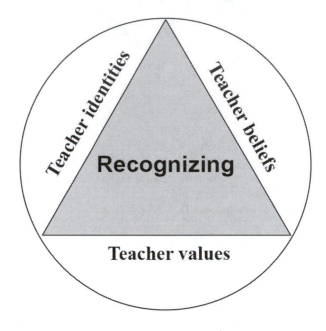

4.1 Teacher Identities

It is beneficial to locate teacher identities within the broader sociological concept of identity, and within the related fields of general education and applied linguistics, and then focus specifically on how the identities of teachers might shape the way they address some of the identity issues confronting them.

4.1.1 The Concept of Identity

Identity has long been a subject of study in fields as varied as anthropology, psychology, sociology, philosophy, theology, and literature. And yet, there is very little consensus among scholars about what really constitutes identity, or how it is actually formed and reformed. As sociologist Anthony Elliott (2009: viii) bemoans, identity "has proved to be one of the most vexing and vexed topics in the social sciences and humanities." One way of trying to understand this vexing subject is by viewing it through the sociological prism of modernism, postmodernism, and globalism (for more details, see Kumaravadivelu 2008, see also Chapter 1 of this book).

To put it briefly, during the days of modernity (roughly covering the period from mid-seventeenth to mid-twentieth century), the individual was largely expected to possess an identity that was in tune with pre-existent and relatively unchanging societal norms. More than anything else, individual identity was tied almost inextricably to affiliation to family and community. Everybody was assigned a neatly designated, hierarchically-coded place under the sun. Furthermore, they were expected to remain there. Individuals encountered an essentialized and totalized concept of identity which treated them as no more than parts of the collective. With socially accepted boundaries of a reified external world imposed on them, individuals had very little meaningful choice outside of clearly delineated characteristics of birth and ethnic origin. If they wanted to find personal meaning, they had to do it within such a rigid system. In other words, the "modern" Self was more externally imposed than self-constructed.

Unlike modernism, the currently prevailing narrative of postmodernism (a period ranging from mid-twentieth century onwards) treats identity as something that is actively constructed by the individual on an on-going basis. It sees identity as fragmented, not unified; multiple, not singular; expansive, not bounded. It bestows a fair degree of agency on the individual in determining a sense of Self. In this view, identity formation is conditioned by several factors including inherited traditions such as ethnicity, external exigencies such as history, ideological constructs such as power, and individual markers such as agency.

The catchword for postmodern identity is *fragmentation*. It captures the epitome of postmodern life. The fragment, according to sociologist Harvie Ferguson

> is not like a splinter of wood or a shard of glass; a piece broken off from an intact and uniform whole. The fragment is a detached portion that takes on a life of its own and may even gain the appearance of self-sufficiency as something *unlike* its parent body.
>
> *(2009: 154, original emphasis)*

The fragmented identity takes on a life of its own through a process of becoming—a process that is continuous, non-linear and unstable. It is less preoccupied with the formation of a durable identity. Instead, it embraces the idea that identity is fluid and amorphous, one that is constantly and endlessly invented and reinvented. It is because of this dynamic and incomplete nature of identity formation that Ferguson characterizes it as "the continuous creation of the fragment; a *bricolage* of the disjointed" (Ibid.: 184, original emphasis).

Compared to modernism, postmodernism has a greater explanatory power to tease out the problematic nature of the concept of Self. However, we need an even broader perspective in order to understand the construction of self-identity in this globalized and globalizing world. This perspective, which may be called *globalism*, is necessitated by fast-evolving global, national, social, and individual realities of the twenty-first century. Globally, our world is marked by a near-collapse of space, time, and borders, resulting in a runaway flow of peoples, goods, and ideas across the world. This phenomenon is aided and accelerated by information revolution, or Internatization. Nationally, people within national borders see unparalleled opportunities for cultural growth as well as unparalleled threats to their national and cultural identity. Globalization has only accentuated the tendency towards tribalization. These opposing processes seem to occur at the same time, the former bringing people together, and the latter pulling them apart.

The social reality presents a picture where ethnic, religious, or linguistic affiliations and affinities within a nation get played up. Each community within a pluralistic society strives to protect and preserve its own identity, resulting not in genuine multiculturalism but in what Amartya Sen (2006) calls *multiple monoculturalisms*. At the individual level, people experience severe pulls and pressures from global, national, and social realities leading to a constant struggle to exercise individual agency in determining a sense of Self. For choosing and forming identities in such a complex environment, individuals require critical knowledge. Using the easily accessible knowledge-base (via the Internet, etc.) and engaging in critical self-reflection, individuals now have the opportunity to evaluate their and others' cultural value systems and develop a global cultural consciousness that has the potential to enrich, and eventually transform, their lives (Kumaravadivelu 2008).

4.1.2 Transforming the Teaching Self

What the above discussion indicates is that teacher identities in a global society are constructed at the complex intersections between individual, social, national and global realities. Teachers everywhere are faced with the challenge of aligning their teaching Self in congruence with contemporary realities while at the same time attempting to transgress any artificial boundaries the realities might impose on them. Teachers' identity formation, then, resides largely in how they make sense of the contemporary realities, and how they negotiate contradictory expectations, and how they derive meaning out of a seemingly chaotic environment.

A crucial factor that will determine whether teachers succeed in forging a desired teaching Self is their ability and willingness to exercise their agency and to formulate strategies of power and resistance. It is true that most teachers operate within a fairly rigid framework of state-sponsored pedagogic policies and practices. However, teaching Self

> is not marked by passivity and conformity, but by a socially engendered reactivity that displays an always present agentive quality.
>
> *(Martin 2007: 87)*

It is the agentive quality that helps teachers recognize that state-sponsored pedagogy is embedded in relations of power and dominance, and is generally aimed at creating and sustaining social inequalities. It is the agentive quality that motivates them to

> develop counterhegemonic pedagogies that not only empower students by giving them the knowledge and social skills they will need to be able to function in the larger society as critical agents, but also educate them for transformative action.
>
> *(Giroux 1988: xxxiii)*

They thus promote conditions of possibility that can function as a catalyst for identity formation and social transformation both for them and for their students (recall the principle of possibility discussed in section 1.2.3).

In exercising their individual agency to form and transform their identities, teachers are not functioning as isolated individuals. Sociologists (e.g., Jenkins 1996) and sociocultural theorists (e.g., Vygotsky 1986) have convincingly argued that identity and agency are notions that are socially constructed and socially shared. "It cannot be otherwise," as Jenkins (1996: 3) argues,

> if only because identities are about meaning, and meaning is not an essential property of words and things. Meanings are always the outcome of agreement or disagreement, always a matter of convention and innovation, always to some extent shared, always to some extent negotiable.

Thus, the teaching Self, like any other Self, is forged through constant negotiations with competing forces. It is the result of individuals' continual critical engagement with others who share their personal and professional space. The shared nature of the creation of teaching Self should not lead us, as Michalinos Zembylas cautions, to the false assumption that

> there is a singular "teacher self" and an essential "teacher identity" as implied in popular cultural myths about teaching.
>
> *(2003: 214)*

On the contrary, teaching Self should be looked at as something unique to the individual. There are several factors that shape the construction of teacher identities, prominent among them are teacher beliefs and teacher values.

4.2 Teacher Beliefs

In this section, I briefly touch upon the psychological construct of beliefs, and how they shape the educational disposition and decision-making on the part of present and prospective teachers.

4.2.1 The Construct of Beliefs

Beliefs are considered to be the driving force behind decisions that individuals make throughout their lives. A belief system is a coherent set of beliefs or precepts that govern one's thoughts, words, and actions. Philosophers and psychologists have long studied belief systems, and yet the construct of beliefs, like the concept of identity, has eluded precise definition. That is because, as Frank Pajares puts it, beliefs

> travel in disguise and often under alias – attitudes, values, judgments, axioms, opinions, ideology, perceptions, conceptions, conceptual systems, preconceptions, dispositions, implicit theories, explicit theories, personal theories, internal mental processes, action strategies, rules of practice, practical principles, per- spectives, repertories of understanding, and social strategy, to name but a few that can be found in the literature.
>
> *(1992: 309)*

Also found in the literature is a persistent attempt to understand what beliefs are. The current understanding is that beliefs are views, propositions, and convictions one dearly holds, consciously or unconsciously, about the truth value of something. They are mostly acquired through such disparate means as personal experiences, familial ties, educational encounters, cultural transmission, or public propagation. Whatever their origin, beliefs are used by individuals as a filtering mechanism through which new encounters and experiences are screened, interpreted, under- stood, and absorbed. They are clearly subjective judgments and may at times defy logic. They are by nature disputable and disposable.

One way of understanding the construct of beliefs is to relate it to knowledge, although it is not easy to separate the two. Educational philosopher John Dewey (1933: 6) indicated the relationship between belief and knowledge when he observed that beliefs

> cover all the matters of which we have no sure knowledge and yet which we are sufficiently confident of to act upon and also the matters that we now accept as certainly true, as knowledge, but which nevertheless may be questioned in the future.

In other words, as Jan Nespor (1987) elaborated later, beliefs can operate indepen- dently of the cognitive reasoning associated with knowledge, and hence, they can be more inconsistent and more inflexible than knowledge systems. They are imbued with strong emotional attachments, and as such they play a crucial role in shaping one's thought, expression, and action. Therefore, what individuals think, say and do may be taken as a reflection of their beliefs. This is true of teachers as well.

4.2.2 Beliefs and Teacher Dispositions

Although philosophers and psychologists have been preoccupied with belief systems for a long time, educationists started engaging in serious and systematic exploration of teacher beliefs only during the 1980s (Fenstermacher 1979, Nespor 1987), and researchers in language teaching (Woods 1996, Borg 2001) followed the lead much later. Ever since, there have been several attempts to discover how beliefs influence teachers and their teaching behavior. Based on a comprehensive review of the literature, Pajares (1992: 324–27) compiled a set of fundamental assumptions about teachers' educational beliefs. Even though this review was carried out nearly two decades ago, the results are still relevant and fundamental, most important of which are:

- Beliefs are formed early and tend to self-perpetuate, persevering even against contradictions caused by reason, time, schooling, or experience;
- The earlier a belief is incorporated into the belief structure, the more difficult it is to alter;
- Individuals tend to hold on to beliefs based on incorrect or incomplete knowledge, even after scientifically correct explanations are presented to them;
- Beliefs about teaching are well established by the time a student teacher enters a teacher education program;
- Teacher beliefs strongly affect teaching behavior, and are instrumental in guiding teachers in defining, selecting, organizing knowledge and information presented to students; and
- By their very nature and origin, some teacher beliefs are more incontrovertible than others.

Clearly, these and other characteristics constitute a loosely-knit teacher belief system that is highly relevant for, and hugely influential in, shaping specific pedagogic decisions that teachers make as part of their practice of everyday teaching.

Turning to some of the specific pedagogic decisions, a detailed case study conducted in the field of general education (Samuelowicz & Bain 2001) focused on two teachers and their beliefs about teaching, knowledge, student learning, and the links between teaching and learning. Teacher A believed firmly in teacher-centered (mostly transmissive) and Teacher B in learner-centered (mostly facilitative) orientations to teaching. An analysis of concrete teaching situations in their classes revealed that Teacher A imparts structured information about his subject matter. Fully in charge, this teacher structured, explained, gave examples, and encouraged very little interaction in class. He passed on his neatly selected and sequenced body of knowledge to his students. He saw "the ability to 'explain it or bring it across to students' as an important characteristic of a good teacher and as his main role" (p. 313).

Teacher B, on the other hand, expected her students to become independent learners and she made it easier for them to achieve this by opening them up to their own possibilities. Using interactive strategies, she helped her students to develop knowledge by unpacking and repacking it, by analyzing and synthesizing it, and by transforming it to make it their own. As a part of her strategy, she also expected her students to keep reflective diaries. The researchers commented that the two teachers' belief orientations reflect their "characteristic perspectives and dispositions to teach in particular ways" (Ibid.: 322). They further concluded that

> the boundary between teaching-centred and learning-centred orientations appears to be relatively "hard" and may require the equivalent of conceptual change (i.e., an accommodative process) to cross it.
>
> *(Ibid.: 322)*

meaning they were very much entrenched in their beliefs.

4.2.3 Language Teacher Beliefs

Not surprisingly, the close connection between teacher beliefs and teacher behavior has been found among English language teachers as well. In a study similar to the one by Samuelowicz and Bain described above, Sue Garton (2008: 67) focused on two TESOL teachers with differing belief systems, and on the differing classroom interactional patterns they promote, and wondered

> how very similar lesson plans carried out by two teachers with totally different beliefs actually lead to formally similar lessons but with very different class atmosphere.

One of her subjects—Charlotte—believed in the personal, affective side of teaching, placing a definite emphasis on people, relationships, and contact. She believed that all she had to do was to create the right conditions, and learning would automatically follow. The other teacher—Linda—focused on her professional competence, subject matter knowledge, and her own preparedness. She thus emphasized the learning process and the need to move the lesson forward methodically. Given these divergent beliefs, their classroom interactional patterns also differed. Linda's classes were "smoother" with a clear Initiation-Response-Feedback (IRF) pattern. Charlotte's IRF sequences were rarely a straightforward three-part exchange, as she promoted negotiated interactions and risk-taking on the part of her learners. Noting that their peers and students considered both of them to be highly effective teachers, Garton derived an important conclusion:

> This means that, as teachers, we will inevitably have different beliefs about teaching and learning and different approaches in the classroom. Concepts such as "best method" and "good teaching" should therefore be abandoned in favour of the recognition of diversity in teachers and the idea that "best teaching" is "the individually best – best step for each teacher."
>
> *(Ibid.: 83)*

Recognition of diversity in teachers entails not only recognizing differential beliefs among different teachers but also recognizing the disparity between teachers' beliefs and their practices. This has been amply illustrated with particular reference to the teaching of grammar in the context of English language teaching. A study of teachers' stated beliefs about the incidental focus on form (which requires primary attention to meaning rather than grammar) and their classroom practices clearly showed inconsistencies between what is believed and what is practiced (Basturkmen, Loewen & Ellis 2004). In a more recent study, Simon Phipps and Simon Borg (2009: 386) examined the disparity in the grammar teaching beliefs and practices of three teachers of English by observing and interviewing them over a period of eighteen months. Their conclusion:

> Prima facie, this study suggests that, in teaching grammar, the beliefs of the three teachers here were not always aligned with their practices.

However, drawing on a familiar distinction between core and peripheral beliefs, they interpreted their findings to mean that the disparity is less in the case of core beliefs and more in the case of peripheral beliefs. In other words, core beliefs are more influential in shaping teachers' instructional strategies, and peripheral beliefs might cause inconsistencies in teacher behavior.

A more unambiguous finding about the disparity between stated beliefs and actual practices comes from Icy Lee (2009) who studied teachers' feedback to student writing in English as a foreign language classrooms. He found several mismatches between beliefs and practices, some of which are (pp. 15–18):

- Teachers pay most attention to language form even though they believe there's more to good writing than grammatical accuracy;
- Teachers mark errors comprehensively even though they believe in selective marking;
- Teachers use error codes although they believe students have a limited ability to decipher them;
- Teachers award scores/grades to student writing although they believe marks/grades draw student attention away from teacher feedback;
- Teachers respond mainly to weaknesses in student writing although they believe that feedback should cover both strengths and weaknesses;
- Teachers think students should learn to take greater responsibility for learning although teachers' feedback practice allows students little room to take control;
- Teachers ask students to do one-shot writing although they think process writing with more drafts is beneficial;
- Teachers continue to mark student writing in the ways they do although they think their effort does not pay off.

Lee stated that he was unable to ascertain whether the mismatches were mere excuses or whether there were justifiable reasons.

Although there is overwhelming evidence that teacher beliefs play a crucial role in shaping teaching performance, it has been widely acknowledged that an individual teacher's belief system does not even require internal consistency and it would indeed be futile to look for it (Pajares 1992). That has not prevented researchers from trying to explain the observed tensions between beliefs and practices in terms of personal and institutional constraints (Farrell & Lim 2005, Phipps & Borg 2009). In looking for plausible explanations, researchers have surmised that some of the tensions may have been the artifacts of the research design they followed; meaning, different elicitation techniques may have elicited different responses. They have further observed that some of the teachers were not consciously aware of their beliefs about teaching until directly asked by the interviewer (Farrell & Lim 2005: 10). In spite of these caveats, researchers have attributed some of the tensions to (a) contextual factors such as a prescribed curriculum, time constraints, and high-stakes examinations; (b) pulls and pressures between teachers' beliefs systems and subsystems (i.e., core vs peripheral beliefs); and (c) reverence and emotional attachments to traditional ways of teaching that they were exposed to when they were students.

What the above discussion indicates is that belief systems have the potential to predispose teachers to take a particular action in the practice of their everyday teaching even if they know it is not the best course of action. This distinct possibility raises questions of moral and ethical import because beliefs "may also become values, which house the evaluative, comparative, and judgmental function ... " that is bound to affect teaching behavior (Pajares 1992: 314). Teacher beliefs are thus closely linked to teacher values.

4.3 Teacher Values

Human values have been a subject of abiding interest from time immemorial, particularly among philosophers and seers. In recent times and in the Western world, American philosopher John Dewey and Canadian philosopher Charles Taylor are among those who have explored the intricacies of human values, making a direct link to education.

For Dewey (1922), education, any education, must be value-based. Values in education are both a means and an end. That is to say, education must be geared towards building a social order that is ethically sound, and it must be done in a way that is morally good. He sees morality essentially as a matter of interactions between individuals and the social environment that they are part of. However, he does seem to put a greater burden on the individual in maintaining high moral standards. Referring to what he considered to be deplorable moral standards that prevailed in his country during his lifetime, he observes (p. 313):

> If the standard of morals is low it is because the education given by the interaction of the individual with his social environment is defective.

One way of rectifying the situation is for the individual to use existing moral standards as tools for critical analysis in order to make appropriate value judgments. If properly done, value judgments made by critically thoughtful individuals can lead to a new course of action which can then be put to the test to see if it effectively addresses the moral defect or not. If it does not, or if new circumstances develop that render the new action inadequate, then, the original appraisal may have to be revisited, reexamined, and recast. By making this recommendation, Dewey is actually expecting the individual to be a moral agent capable of proactive and productive response.

Agreeing with and expanding on Dewey's emphasis on the individual's moral agency, Taylor (1994: 3) states that

> values education, in its various forms, encourages reflection on choices, exploration of opportunities and commitment to responsibilities, and for the individual in society, to develop values preferences and an orientation to guide attitudes and behaviour.

But, unlike Dewey, Taylor makes a more nuanced argument about the relationship between the individual and the social in shaping the individual's or the society's value system. He acknowledges, more explicitly than Dewey does, that values are deeply embedded in a pre-existing social environment, and that languages and cultures play a crucial role in shaping one's moral values. What the social environment provides us all with is "something so basic and inescapable to us as a sense of identity depends on taking some goods seriously" (Taylor 1994: 206). Common good, that is.

A close interpretation of Taylor's ideas on values yields the following (Reckling 2001): (a) values are intrinsic to human life because human life is basically oriented towards common good; (b) human languages are penetrated by moral judgments, with commonly used words such as *good* and *evil*, *right* and *wrong*, etc.; (c) values are disclosed through people's life-worldly perspective and performance; (d) values and the discourse on values are relational and culturally-laden; and yet (e) certain basic values are universally valid.

Taylor is quite clear that the culturally-embedded and universally valid nature of values does not absolve the individual from maintaining, and if need be, modifying values because values would not exist without agents or valuers. Like Dewey, he also calls for critical reflection on the part of the individual, but distinguishes between *engaged* and *disengaged* reflection. The first entails a close scrutiny of values requiring a mastery of evaluative skills that allow one to be open to new insights thereby enabling one to make appropriate value judgments. The second entails stepping back, gaining distance to the case at hand and comparing it to other similar and different cases from a dispassionate perspective before making value judgments. Either way, one exercises one's moral agency to clarify, modify or solidify one's considered conviction to values.

In spite of the subtle differences in the way they approach the relationship between the individual and the social, both Dewey and Taylor place enormous responsibility on the shoulders of teachers, most of whom are faced with onerous social and institutional constraints. They both adhere to a useful distinction, made originally by Dewey, between "the teaching of morality" and "the morality of teaching"—the former referring to moral instruction given to students, and the latter to what the teachers (should) do in the classrooms. They both give greater importance to the latter. They have inspired several educators who have expanded on the idea of the morality of teaching and have helped us understand it better.

4.3.1 The Morality of Teaching

In an inspiring book titled *Exploring the Moral Heart of Teaching*, David Hansen (2001) observes that teaching is, and has always been, a moral activity. Drawing our attention to the long and rich tradition behind the idea of teaching as a moral and intellectual practice, he emphasizes the need for teachers to develop a sense of tradition about the values of teaching and to let that tradition animate their consciousness. Hansen sees "the dynamic human element" as constituting the center of this moral and intellectual activity, and, therefore, good teaching is one that

> involves enriching, not impoverishing, students' understandings of self, others, and the world. It means expanding, not contracting, students' knowledge, insights, and interests. It means deepening, not rendering more shallow, students' ways of thinking and feeling. And it entails paying intellectual and moral attention as a teacher.
>
> *(Ibid.: ix)*

A teacher *is* a moral agent. It is a secret hidden in plain sight. Almost everything a teacher does, has the potential to carry a moral import because "the place we call school is an environment of moral interaction and sometimes moral struggle" (Nash 2005: 4). A teacher's moral agency is revealed in myriad ways: in the selection of textbooks, in the way curricular content knowledge is re-structured and re-presented, in the use of instructional strategies, in the choice of classroom interactional patterns, in the way classroom activities are organized, in the teaching style, in cultivating student relations, in responding to conflicts generated by students and peers, etc.

In carrying out their myriad roles and responsibilities, teachers are often confronted with a seemingly difficult choice between caring for their students and abiding by rules they are expected to enforce. For instance, it has been reported that teachers in certain California schools knowingly subvert an official state government policy that prohibits them from using bilingual teaching by surreptitiously practicing it because they are convinced that their limited English proficiency students, who are mostly recent immigrants, require bilingual teaching in order to succeed in their studies (Varghese 2001, cited in Johnston 2003). The teachers in this case deliberately made a moral decision to put more trust in their own value judgment and in their conscience rather than in rules imposed on them by an uncaring system. Cases like this present what educationists have termed a conflict between care and justice in teacher ethics.

The not-so-apparent disparity between care and justice has been succinctly captured by Virginia Held (2006: 15):

> An ethic of justice focuses on questions of fairness, equality, individual rights, abstract principles, and the consistent application of them. An ethic of care focuses on attentiveness, trust, responsiveness to need, narrative nuance, and cultivating caring relations.

In attempting to resolve potential conflicts between the ethics of care and the ethics of rules, teachers may have to navigate a minefield of conflicting institutional and individual interests. In order to strike a judicious balance, they may have to "organize care and distribute it justly. Conversely, they must ensure that justice is meted out caringly" (Colnerud 2006: 369).

"Care picks up where justice leaves off"—is an astute observation from feminist educationist Nel Noddings (1999: 16). She has elaborated the observation into what is called a care theory that "may provide us with a powerful approach to ethics and moral education in this age of globalization" (Noddings 2010: 390). An important aspect of care ethics is that they are neither collective nor individual; they are relational. The collective derives its power from communitarian ethics and may blind us to problems of individuals, particularly those of outsiders. The individual may approach rights and freedom with an evangelical zeal and consider themself superior enough to impose their values on others. The relational, on the other hand, helps us to listen attentively to others without prejudice. In a caring relation, Noddings (Ibid.: 390) tells us,

> the carer is first of all attentive to the cared-for, and this attention is receptive; that is, the carer puts aside her own values and projects, and tries to understand the expressed needs of the cared-for.

Under this congenial atmosphere, sympathy toward the cared-for generates "a willingness to listen and be moved" (Ibid.: 392). Clearly, care theory sheds useful light on "the dynamic human element" neglected by justice and rule-governed practices of rigid educational systems.

A relational approach to caring is what is most needed when teachers deal with students from linguistically and culturally diverse backgrounds. Teachers of English in particular, because they are dealing with a language of globality and coloniality, face numerous dilemmas and conflicts almost on a regular basis. Rightly pointing out that *all* aspects of English language teaching "are imbued with values and moral meaning" (p. x), Bill Johnston (2003), in his book *Values in English Language*

Teaching, offers several interesting cases and useful insights. He talks about his own dilemma when he noticed a clear case of plagiarism perpetrated by a Korean student. Faced with a choice between punishing her, as he is expected to do according to University regulations, and following his own moral values about mentoring a foreign student who badly needed help with American academic expectations, he chose the latter. He also talks about his friend, Peter, who was teaching English to Palestinian and Jordanian students in Jordan. After many agonizing moments, Peter decided to reverse his earlier decision to fail a Palestinian student from the occupied West Bank because failing that student would have meant forcing him to return to Israel and face devastating consequences and diminished career opportunities. In these and other cases, Johnston persuades us to see how "in the decision-making processes of teaching, somewhere along the road rationality ceases to operate effectively" (p. 8).

On a broader level, teachers of English have been alerted to the political economy of English language teaching, and how it directly or indirectly influences our professional practices that raise several moral dilemmas. Specifically, teachers have been cautioned

- that "there are major commercial interests involved in the global English language industry" (Phillipson 2003: 16);
- that the practices associated with English language testing conducted at the global level (e.g., TOEFL—Test of English as a Foreign Language) are "undemocratic and unethical" (Shohamy 1998: 340);
- that the teaching of English is being (mis)used for missionary purposes under the false pretense of promoting much needed developmental projects (Edge 2003);
- that there exists a dangerous liaison between the forces of globalization, empire, and TESOL, and, as a result, English language teachers "knowingly or unknowingly, play a role in the service of global corporations and imperial powers" (Kumaravadivelu 2006a: 1); and
- that teachers of English "cooperate in their own marginalization" if they continue to see themselves only as *language* teachers without paying serious attention to social and political issues that impact on the practice of their everyday teaching (Gee 1994: 190).

What the above observations implore the language teachers to do is to systematically analyze, understand, and activate their own intellectual and moral agency; in short, interrogate their teaching Self.

4.4 Interrogating the Teaching Self

As stated at the beginning of this chapter, achieving desirable goals in teaching depends on the kind of teaching Self that teachers bring with them, and understanding the teaching Self is all about understanding one's identities, beliefs, and values. Present and prospective teachers can systematically interrogate and critically interpret their own teaching Self by using critical autoethnography as an investigative tool.

Drawn from anthropological tradition, and popularized by cultural studies theorist Mary Louise Pratt (1992) and others who originally explored the complexities of Self and the Other in the context of colonial and postcolonial studies, auto-ethnography involves introspective accounts of individuals who are interested in exploring their inner Self associated with their lived experience in personal and professional domains. By playing the role of a participant observer, they try to fathom their inner Self and attempt to get to grips with their own identities, beliefs, values, attitudes, thoughts, feelings, prejudices, etc. An autoethnographical study is therefore one's subjective analysis and assessment of one's Self but done in a systematic and sustained manner, and as such, it is concerned more with interpretable thoughts than with irrefutable facts. The chief goal is self-realization, with attendant possibilities for self-reconstruction and self-revitalization.

A word about the "critical" dimension of autoethnography is in order here. It is, in part, influenced by the logic of critical pedagogy advocated by Paulo Freire. It compels teachers to see schools and colleges as not simply instructional sites but as "cultural arenas where heterogeneous ideological, discursive, and social forms collide in an unremitting struggle for dominance" (McLaren 1995b: 30). Following the Freirean perspective, teachers reflect on and review their lived experience and find ways to challenge the social and historical forces that under-mine their and their students' self-actualization. They develop sociopolitical con-sciousness and learn to be assertive in acting upon this consciousness, thereby stretching their role beyond the borders of the classroom. They come to view a critical autoethnographic study not merely as a means for maximizing learning opportunities in the classroom but also as a mechanism for transforming their identities, beliefs, and values.

Teachers will be able to conduct a viable critical autoethnographic study primarily through self-observation, self-analysis and self-reflection. They collect data about their identities, beliefs and values from as many sources as possible, including notes from personal conversations with peers and students, formal interviews with people associated with their personal and professional life, personally generated materials such as reflective journals, diary entries, etc. They then describe, interpret, and explain the data, returning to the same piece of data again and again adding different layers of analysis as and when new encounters and experiences are available. Through this self-observational, self-reflective process, teachers construct their self-image of who they are as persons and who they are as professionals. Gradually, they sketch a self-portrait that renders the connection between the personal, the professional, the pedagogical, and the political visible to themselves and to others. The self-portrait takes the form of narrative stories.

Narrating personal stories is a commonplace human activity. We live by narratives, that is, "we dream in narrative, daydream in narrative, remember, anticipate, hope, despair, plan, revise, criticize, gossip, learn, hate and love by narrative" (Hardy 1968: 5, cited in Pavlenko 2007). General educationists (e.g., Connelly & Clandinin 1990) as well as applied linguists (e.g., Johnson & Golombek eds. 2002) have advocated the use of narrative inquiry to help teachers understand and articulate their identities, beliefs, and values. Based on their personal experience, Clandinin and Connelly (2000: 18) report that

> narrative is the best way of representing and understanding experience. Experience is what we study, and we study it narratively because narrative thinking is a key form of experience and a key way of writing and thinking about it.

Johnson and Golembek, researching and writing in the context of TESOL, reiterate the same view when they point out that

> inquiry into experience enables teachers to act with foresight. It gives them increasing control over their thoughts and actions; grants their experiences enriched, deepened meaning; and enables them to be more thoughtful of their work.
>
> *(2002: 6–7)*

While there is hardly any dispute that critical autoethnography-based narrative inquiry significantly raises teachers' consciousness about their teaching Self, and equally significantly helps them reshape their identities, beliefs and values, serious doubts have been raised about their ability to articulate their inner thoughts. For instance, Graham Crookes (2009: 16), using the term "philosophy of teaching" to refer to teachers' narratives, observes:

> Many of the teachers I work with comment that they find developing and/or articulating their philosophy of teaching to be difficult, even though they may be somewhat experienced as teachers and even though they may be presently teaching.

He goes on to point out that even teachers who may have internalized their own philosophy of teaching do not get the distance that may be needed to articulate their thoughts. Roumi Ilieva (2010) raises yet another concern. There is a distinct possibility that teacher's narratives about their teaching Self may not be any more than a mere "ventriloquation of authoritative discourses" (p. 355). That is, teachers may uncritically repeat the views and voices of scholars they read in various courses in their teacher education program.

While I share these legitimate concerns, I contend that if most of the present and prospective teachers have difficulty in thinking narratively and in articulating their thoughts sharply, it is by no small measure due to current teacher education programs that seldom impart the knowledge, skills, and disposition necessary for teachers to perform critical authoethnography. What we need to do is to familiarize our teachers with the basics of critical autoethnography so that they learn to use authoritative discourses introduced to them as a springboard to induce their own critical thinking. Or, to put it differently

> only through the establishment of discursive knowledge/power relations in TESOL classrooms that systematically invite students' voices can we hope to open up possibilities for students' agentive, dialogical appropriation of program discourses.
>
> *(Ilieva 2010: 362)*

There are several ways in which teacher educators can open up possibilities for their student teachers. Some of the reflective tasks and exploratory projects that I have presented in this book and in my earlier work (Kumaravadivelu 2003b) provide illustrative examples. I have found it generally useful to (a) present case studies of experienced teachers that highlight the inner struggle they have gone through and the strategies they have followed to overcome them; (b) design problem-posing tasks that help student teachers question their own long-cherished, not fully thought through beliefs and assumptions; (c) provide them with real or constructed critical incidents about what is and what is not acceptable in a classroom environment and ask them to make and defend the value-judgment they would have made in that situation; (d) require them to maintain detailed journal entries representing their stream of consciousness response to the issues they read about and discuss in class; and (e) encourage them to use the popular social media to exchange their evolving identities, beliefs, and values with their peers in order to have a meaningful and critical dialogue with them.

In order to reach out to those teachers who might feel diffident or challenged, Gary Barkhuizen and Rosemary Wette (2008) have suggested the use of what they call narrative frames. The idea is to give student teachers an open-ended, loosely-structured outline prompting them to think about a particular episode or experience and write a coherent narrative. Here is a suggested narrative frame (p. 385):

> I remember once in my classroom I had a very difficult time trying to −.
> The main reason for this problem was that −.
> I tried to solve the problem by −.
> It would have been very helpful if −.
> In relation to this difficulty, the type of research I'd like to do would −.
> The aim of the research would be to −.
> A major constraint, though, might be that −.

Such narrative frames are deemed to

enable the teachers to write narratively by scaffolding them through the specially designed narrative structure, and they encourage reflection because of the nature of what they are required to write

(Ibid.: 381).

There is merit in using narrative frames as a first step to help novice teachers overcome any initial reticence on their part but the frames should not limit their thinking and expression. Care should also be taken to make sure that temporary scaffolding does not become a permanent crutch.

4.5 In Closing

In this chapter, I focused on crucial issues that current language teacher education has almost completely neglected until very recently: identities, beliefs, and values. I stressed the need for both the language teacher and the language teacher educator to recognize the vital role played by these rather imprecise human attributes in determining the effectiveness of everyday teaching. I pointed out that teachers can not simply make sense of their teaching Self unless they fully understand their own identities, beliefs, and values. In order to put these attributes in broader philosophical, psychological, and sociological perspective, I briefly outlined the concepts of identity and identity formation, beliefs, and belief systems, and values and value judgments. I then connected these general concepts to specific pedagogic imperatives drawing insights from general education as well as from the field of English language teaching.

The challenges facing student teachers, practicing teachers and teacher educators are many, and are becoming increasingly complicated because of the demands of a global society with its linguistic and cultural pulls and pressures. Teachers have to learn to recognize and renew not only their own identities, beliefs and values but also strive to shape those of their learners as well. They have to learn to interrogate their teaching Self using critical autoethnography as an investigative tool, and draw a self-portrait connecting the personal, the professional, the pedagogical, and the political. A responsible teacher education program aided by responsive teacher educators can make that happen.

Rapid Reader Response

Write a quick response to the following questions. Form small groups, share your thoughts and discuss them with other members of the group.

1   What is the one big point you learned from this chapter?
2   What is the one main unanswered question you leave the chapter with?
3   What is the one surprising idea or concept you encountered in this chapter?
4   What is one example of terminology or concept you do not fully understand?

Reflective Tasks

Task 4.1 Transformation and Transgression

T4.1.1 Think about this passage from the chapter: " … teacher identities in a global society are constructed at the complex intersections between individual, social, national, and global realities. Teachers everywhere are faced with the challenge of aligning their teaching Self in congruence with contemporary realities while at the same time attempting to transgress any artificial boundaries the realities might impose on them." Respond to the following questions from your perspective as a student-teacher or a practicing teacher, depending on who you are.

T4.1.2 Select any one of the four contemporary realities and think about how it affects your personal identity as a student-teacher (or a teacher).

T4.1.3 Specifically, what do you think you have to do to align your teaching Self with the reality you selected?

T4.1.4 In what way might the reality you selected impose any artificial boundaries and limitations on you in your attempt to realize the full potential of your teaching Self?

T4.1.5 What are the ways in which you can exercise your agency to transgress those boundaries and limitations?

Task 4.2 Beliefs and Knowledge

T4.2.1 We learned in this chapter that beliefs can operate independently of the cognitive reasoning associated with knowledge, and that teachers do follow certain beliefs about teaching even though cognitively they may not make much sense. Reflect on this statement.

T4.2.2 Can you think of one specific belief of yours (as a student-teacher or as a practicing teacher) that you have steadfastly adhered to because of emotional, not rational, reasons?

T4.2.3 Think about how that belief and the attendant classroom behavior may have affected your relations with your peers and teachers.

T4.2.4 Have a critical conversation with yourself and try to explain to yourself why the emotional aspect of your belief has to override the rational aspect of it.

T4.2.5 Explain your belief and behavior to a friendly peer and try to justify it. See whether that person agrees or disagrees with your justification.

Task 4.3 Narration and Nuisance

T4.3.1 Consider this: Narrating personal stories is a commonplace human activity. We live by narratives, that is, "we dream in narrative, daydream in narrative, remember, anticipate, hope, despair, plan, revise, criticize, gossip, learn, hate and love by narrative" (Hardy 1968: 5, cited in Pavlenko 2007).

T4.3.2 If narrating personal stories is a commonplace human activity, why do you think many student teachers and practicing teachers find it so difficult to tell stories about their own teaching Self?

T4.3.3 We learn that even experienced teachers who may have internalized their own philosophy of teaching have not been able to clearly articulate their thoughts. Why do you think that is the case?

T4.3.4 Do you agree that, when pressed to do a critical authoethnography, student teachers uncritically repeat the views and voices of scholars they read in various courses in their teacher education program? Why? Why not?

T4.3.5 What specific pedagogic strategies do you think teacher preparation programs should introduce and implement in order to help student teachers become confident and competent narrators of their own teaching Self?

Exploratory projects

Project 4.1 Teacher Beliefs

We learned in this chapter that teacher beliefs strongly influence teaching behavior. This project is aimed at helping you to explore the beliefs of one of your teachers (if you are a student-teacher) or a colleague (if you are a practicing teacher) focusing narrowly on one aspect of his/her teaching, namely, classroom interactional style. (Feel free to choose any other aspect of classroom teaching style such as instructional strategies, curricular goals, student relations, conflict resolution, etc. If you do, stick to that one aspect throughout this project.)

P4.1.1 Think and write a brief account of your beliefs (either as a student-teacher, or as a practicing teacher) about the classroom interactional style that you think you follow (or would like to follow). Think also about the source(s) and evolution of those beliefs.

P4.1.2 Select a teacher or a colleague who is willing to participate in this project. Based on your familiarity, write a profile of his/her teaching style as you perceive it.

P4.1.3 Interview the selected person to seek his/her perspective on personal teaching style and the fundamental beliefs governing it.

P4.1.4 Find out whether he/she believes in a teacher-centered (mostly transmissive) or a learner-centered (mostly facilitative) orientation to teaching; and whether he/she follows an IRF (Initiation-Response-Feedback) sequence or an open-ended, negotiated interaction in class. Do you see any connection between their orientation and their beliefs? If so, what?

P4.1.5 Find out about possible sources of his/her belief (i.e., teacher education program, professional literature, teaching experience, etc.).

P4.1.6 Find out whether the stated beliefs have been held steadfastly or have been changing from time to time, and if so, what might be the reasons.

P4.1.7   Ask whether he/she has been actually practicing what he/she believes as far as classroom interactional pattern is concerned, and find out possible reasons for any self-acknowledged discrepancies (i.e., institutional, curricular, or other, constraints).

P4.1.8   Compare the profile you put together about this person and the profile that emerged in your informal study. What are the similarities and dissimilarities, and how might you account for them?

P4.1.9   Reflect on and briefly write about what you learned from doing this project, and how it might contribute to a reassessment of your own beliefs.

Project 4.2 Learner Identities

This chapter focuses, in part, on teacher identities. What has not been addressed in the chapter is how teachers "read" and respond to fragments of learner identities they constantly encounter in their classroom.

A stereotypical classroom identity that is normally attributed to learners of English from Asian countries is that they are very reticent and do not actively participate in class discussions (for details, see Kumaravadivelu 2008, Chapter 4 on Cultural stereotype and its perils). A Vietnamese scholar, Le Ha Phan (2007), investigated how classroom interactional patterns followed in Australian Universities would affect the classroom identity formation and perception of a group of experienced Vietnamese teachers of English who were studying there for their Masters degree in TESOL.

Phan's ethnographic study revealed that, compared to white Australian students, his Vietnamese subjects were mostly silent in class. One of his subjects, Trang, shared his perception, as gathered from Phan's report (pp. 26–28): (a) Australian students ask questions just to attract the lecturer's attention even though many of their questions are "nonsense, funny and ridiculous" and they are chiefly aimed at pleasing the lecturers who favor those students who ask questions in class; (b) Vietnamese students, both in Vietnam and while in Australia, think about and ask only questions that are "heavy-weight enough to ask," and do not "challenge teachers or test their ability" without solid reason.

Phan observes that both Australian lecturers and students and Vietnamese students tend to focus on perceived identity differences. He further notes that "they identified themselves by defining others" (Ibid.: 27). He recommends orientation programs before, during and after a course where the participants can "express and exchange their perceptions of their identities" (Ibid.: 33).

Now, use this background information to do the following project.

P4.2.1   Reflect on your views of classroom participation. Did you as a student actively participate in class discussions? Do you now, as a student-teacher or as a teacher, demand active participation from yourself, from your classmates, or from your students?

P4.2.2 Briefly write down your response to what Phan reported on Vietnamese student teachers. What do you think about Trang's perception of Australian and Vietnamese students and their classroom interaction?

P4.2.3 Share the Phan report summarized above with a group of classmates (or peers) who are native speakers of English. Ask them, individually, for their reaction to Trang's perception of Australian and Vietnamese students.

P4.2.4 Share the Phan report with a group of classmates (or peers) who are non-native speakers of English, preferably from Asia. Ask them, individually, for their reaction to Trang's perception of Australian and Vietnamese students and their classroom interaction.

P4.2.5 Arrange for a group discussion among the participants. See whether, as a group, you can come to a consensus about the best way of recognizing and respecting cultural identity expectations that participants (both teachers and students) bring to the classroom.

P4.2.6 How would you and your group respond to a possible criticism that it is one thing to adhere to a particular classroom interactional behavior in one's country but it is another matter to neglect to learn the cultural expectations of an educational institution in a host country? That is, it is in the educational interest of Vietnamese students to learn to actively participate in classroom interaction at least while they are studying in a country like Australia.

P4.2.7 Again in your group, share your views on how teacher identities and expectations can shape the way you (and teacher educators) "read" and respond to learner identities and expectations.

P4.2.8 Write a brief statement on what you learned from doing this project.

Project 4.3 Care Justice

This project is aimed at finding out how you and your peers will respond to a moral dilemma and try to balance care and justice in exercising the authority vested in a teacher.

P4.3.1 Recall the episodes involving California teachers who defied a state law about bilingual education, Johnston who defied his University rules regarding plagiarism, and Peter who reversed his decision to fail a Palestinian student.

P4.3.2 Think about how you would have responded if you were a decision-maker involved in those episodes. Write a brief three-part statement describing the episodes, explaining your decision, and defending it.

P4.3.3 Select a classmate or a colleague and share your statement with him/her. Ask your partner to write a brief response commenting on your decision agreeing or disagreeing with you.

P4.3.4 Select an administrator in your institution who is entrusted with the task of enforcing rules and regulations, and share your statement with him/her. Solicit a critical response from this person.

P4.3.5 Have a conversation with your partner and the administrator. If the views diverge, talk about the rationale behind the divergence, and see whether you can convince them (or be convinced by them). If the views converge, talk about the moral dilemma and inner struggle you all may have gone through in the process of balancing care and justice.

P4.3.6 Think about what you learned from doing this project.

5

DOING

My argument is that there need not be a 'doer behind the deed,' but that the 'doer' is variably constructed in and through the deed.

(Judith Butler 1990: 142)

5.0 Introduction

If the previous chapter dealt more with the doer than with the doing, this chapter deals more with the doing than with the doer. The knowing of professional, personal, and procedural knowledge, the analyzing of learner needs, motivation, and autonomy, and the recognizing of teacher identities, beliefs, and values will all come close to naught if the doer is not doing. The doing part of the teacher consists of three componential parts: teaching that promotes desired learning outcome, theorizing that involves deriving a personal theory of practice, and dialogizing that seeks critical conversations with informed interlocutors as well as with one's evolving teaching Self. As this chapter develops, it will become clear that these three components are closely linked to the three operating principles of particularity, practicality, and possibility discussed in Chapter 1. It will also be clear that one of the primary goals of any teacher education program must be to prepare teachers who are successful in doing teaching, theorizing, and dialogizing.

5.1 Teaching

Teaching has been defined variously by various players. There are those who believe that teaching is no more than channeling the flow of content information from one end of the educational spectrum (i.e., the expert) to the other (i.e., the learner) with the teacher merely being a conduit. There are those who believe that

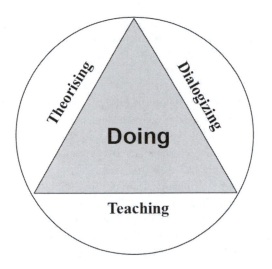

teaching is an intellectual activity grounded in reflective thought processes involving creativity, artistry, and context-sensitivity. And then there are those who believe that teaching should aim at a much nobler task of striving not only for educational advancement of learners but also for the personal transformation of learners and teachers. In accordance with these expectations, a teacher's role has been described as that of a passive technician, a reflective practitioner, or a transformative intellectual. Instead of going into the details of these teacher roles (see Kumaravadivelu 2003b, Chapter 1 for details), I shall focus on the twin proposition that the doing of teaching in the language classroom chiefly entails (a) maximizing learning opportunities and (b) mentoring personal transformation.

5.1.1 Maximizing Learning Opportunities

Unquestionably, the central goal of teaching is to assist learners in their attempt to realize their fullest learning potential. The doing of teaching must therefore be aimed at creating the conditions necessary for that to occur in as efficient a manner and in as short a time as possible. However, the effectiveness of teaching depends to a considerable extent on the learners' willing cooperation to make use of the conditions created by the teacher. It is because of this collaborative nature of learning and teaching that Dick Allwright (1986: 6) defines teaching as "the interactive process whereby learning opportunities are created." This definition avoids designating a provider; that is to say, both teachers and learners can create and utilize learning opportunities thereby jointly contributing to the effective management of learning.

If management of learning in the classroom is a joint endeavor between teachers and learners, then,

> we may have to get away from the long-cherished notion that pedagogic success is determined by a combination of a well-planned teachers' agenda supported by a well-designed textbook based on a well-conceived syllabus.
>
> *(Kumaravadivelu 2003b: 45)*

Instead, we should be focusing more on the creation and utilization of learning opportunities in class unfettered and undeterred by the limitations imposed by teaching related aids such as pre-determined syllabi, textbooks, or lesson plans. It is in this connection that Allwright (2005: 16) cautions us against any over-reliance on pre-meditated *teaching points*, because they not only leave out the learner altogether but also misrepresent "the relationship between teaching and learning, suggesting that what matters is that things get 'taught,' not that they get 'learned.'" He goes on to say that without necessarily abandoning teaching points altogether, we should think in terms of enriching learning opportunities. In other words, it is not sufficient if teaching creates learning opportunities but it should also create learning opportunities that are of high quality.

Operationalizing and achieving quality is by far the most demanding part of creating language learning opportunities in class, according to David Crabbe (2003). He argues that, in spite of the difficulties involved, there are two compelling reasons for taking up the challenge: one is "the weakening of the concept of method" (p. 15). The current postmethod environment (see section 1.1.5 for more) encourages us to move away from the traditional framework of quality associated with "*the method* and its prescribed procedures" (Ibid.: 15, his emphasis) leading to the opening up of autonomy for teachers to reflect on and ensure quality teaching in their own context. The second is the globalization of education (see section 1.1. for more) "leading to processes of benchmarking and evaluation to achieve international recognition of quality, whether for purposes of accountability or commerce" (Ibid.: 16). He recommends an opportunity framework in language teaching that encourages "teachers and learners to work from basic principles rather than fixed routines" because a

> thinking teacher or learner is primarily a problem solver following a heuristic path to identify the appropriate learning opportunities to reach the intended learning goals.
>
> *(Ibid.: 31)*

One such framework that does provide "basic principles rather than fixed routines" is the macrostrategic framework proposed within the parameters of a postmethod pedagogy (Kumaravadivelu 2003b). It consists of ten basic principles derived from historical, theoretical, empirical, and experiential insights related to language learning and teaching. It entreats teachers to

- maximize learning opportunities so that they can strike a balance between their role as managers of teaching acts and their role as mediators of learning acts;
- minimize perceptual mismatches so that they can address potential mismatches between teacher intentions and learner interpretations;

- facilitate negotiated interaction so that they can empower and encourage learners to initiate topic and talk, not just react and respond;
- promote learner autonomy so that they can equip learners with strategic means necessary to self-direct and self-monitor their own learning;
- foster language awareness so that they can draw learners' attention to the formal and functional properties of their L2 in order to increase the degree of explicitness required to promote L2 learning;
- activate intuitive heuristics so that they can help learners to infer and internalize underlying rules governing grammatical usage and communicative use;
- contextualize linguistic input so that they can highlight how language usage and use are shaped by linguistic, extralinguistic, situational, and extrasituational contexts;
- integrate language skills so that they can show learners how listening, speaking, reading, and writing function in an integrated fashion;
- ensure social relevance so that they can be sensitive to the societal, political, economic, and educational environment in which learning and teaching take place; and
- raise cultural consciousness so that they can engage their learners in a process of classroom participation that puts a premium on their power/knowledge.

Using these macrostrategies as guiding principles, teachers will be able to design interactive classroom activities that are context-specific as well as quality-sensitive (see Kumaravadivelu 2003b for illustrative examples).

The quality of learning opportunity created in the classroom is closely related to whether teachers see their roles as passive technicians, reflective practitioners, or transformative intellectuals. Of particular interest and importance is their role as transformative intellectuals, which prompts them to view teaching not merely as a mechanism for maximizing learning opportunities in the classroom but also as a means for personal transformation.

5.1.2 Mentoring Personal Transformation

As noted earlier, the idea of teachers as transformative intellectuals evolved out of seminal thoughts from the Brazilian philosopher of education, Paulo Freire. In all his writings (1972 and elsewhere), he tirelessly espouses the cause of sociopolitical emancipation and individual empowerment through the democratic process of education. For him, education is nothing if not liberating. For that reason, he rejects the traditional teacher-fronted pedagogy that merely transmits content information, describing it as something that turns learners into containers,

> into receptacles to be filled by the teacher. The more completely he fills the receptacles, the better a teacher he is. The more meekly the receptacles permit themselves to be filled, the better students they are.
>
> *(1972: 45)*

To counter this banking system of education, he advocates *conscientization*, a process by which individuals develop critical consciousness of a heightened level so that they become acutely aware not only of the socio, political, and historical forces that are arraigned against them but also of the imperative need to recognize their own agency and act on it for individual and social good. "Conscientization," Freire (1989: 46) explains,

> is not exactly the starting point of commitment. Conscientization is more of a product of commitment. I do not have to be already critically self-conscious in order to struggle. By struggling I become conscious/aware.

Critical engagement is a sure path that opens to genuine personal transformation.

Friere's call for personal transformation through education has resonated immensely with general educationists who have, for nearly a quarter of a century, solidified his ideas into what has come to be known as critical pedagogy. At a broad level, critical pedagogists seek to help teachers cultivate their students' intellect so that they can enhance their socioeconomic mobility and also their sociopolitical presence. At a more practical level, critical pedagogists design appropriate curricula and classroom activities that facilitate pedagogical interactions between macro level factors such as linguistic, cultural, political, and social dynamics, and micro level lived experiences that teachers and students bring with them to the classroom. Through problem-posing activities, they help students problematize familiar and taken for granted issues so that students can perceive and interpret them from a critical perspective. By doing so, they try to "empower students by giving them the knowledge and social skills they will need to be able to function in the larger society as critical agents, but also educate them for transformative action" (Giroux 1988: xxxiii). In such a scenario, critical pedagogy becomes "not a means to prepare students for the world of subordinated labor or 'careers,' but a preparation for a self-managed life" (Aronowitz 2009: ix).

Although the field of education has been actively pursuing critical pedagogy for a considerable period of time, it is only during the 1990s that the field of TESOL took a decidedly critical turn. Ever since, there has been a growing realization that any personal transformation has to be affected, in part, by using language as a medium and therefore language teaching and language teachers bear a special responsibility. It is now fairly clear among a large segment of English language teachers that critical pedagogy, as Kumaravadivelu summarizes,

> is about connecting the word with the world. It is about recognizing language as ideology, not just as system. It is about extending the educational space to the social, cultural, and political dynamics of language use, not just limiting it to the phonological, syntactic, and pragmatic domains of language usage.

(2006c: 70)

It is also about exploiting linguistic resources to create the cultural forms and interested knowledge that give meaning to the lived experiences of teachers and learners. With that realization has come the understanding that language teaching is more than teaching language.

Several scholars in the field of English language teaching have advocated the use of critical pedagogic principles and practices. In an early exploration, Elsa Auerbach (1992) has proposed five simple steps to critically engage students in problem-posing activities in the context of adult ESL literacy: (a) describe a cultural text (a code) related to a problem pertaining to learners' lived experiences; (b) ask questions to help students identify and clarify the problem; (c) ask them to share similar experiences; (d) help them analyze the root causes of the problem; and finally (e) help them strategize possible responses. Brian Morgan (1998) has demonstrated how even in teaching units of language as system, such as phonological and grammatical features, the values of critical practice and community development can be profitably employed. Sarah Benesch (2001) has suggested ways and means of linking the linguistic text and sociopolitical context with the larger community for the purpose of turning classroom input and interaction into effective instruments of personal transformation. In short, advocates of critical approaches to English language teaching have clearly shown that

> language is not simply a means of expression or communication; rather, it is a practice that constructs, and is constructed by, the ways language learners understand themselves, their social surroundings, their histories, and their possibilities for the future.
>
> *(Norton & Toohey 2004: 1)*

Globalization has opened up new possibilities and challenges for critical pedagogic practices in English language teaching. We saw in Chapter 3 how the expanding global cultural consciousness is demanding that English language teachers develop their students' critical awareness of contemporary realities that challenge their needs, their autonomy, and their motivation. According to Noah De Lissovoy, this global development has created the need for what he calls a *critical pedagogy of the global* that

> must be able to reckon with the fundamental transformations of consciousness, experience, and identity that are central to the shift to the historical condition of globality.
>
> *(2009: 191)*

What this means is that language teachers have to offer their students a new perspective and a new way of thinking about the social, political, and cultural factors that shape their identity formation and personal transformation.

So far, I touched upon how the doing of teaching entails the twin task of maximizing learning opportunities and mentoring personal transformation. A legitimate concern that has been raised is whether teachers might not find it too challenging to develop necessary knowledge and skills to successfully carry out the task. In this context, Gustavo Fischman (2009: 210) brings our attention to "potentially transformative characteristics that are already present in many teachers, even if those are formulated in naïve forms or in commonsense terms." Many thoughtful teachers are already sensitive to linguistic, cultural, and educational demands of the global society. In fact, they are constantly involved in critical mind engagement. Their success and the satisfaction they derive from it depends largely on the quality of their mind engagement. One way of enhancing the quality of their mind engagement is for them to recognize the importance of theorizing.

5.2 Theorizing

Perhaps nothing has generated so much sound and so little light as the discourse on theory, research and practice in TESOL. "Theory failed," asserts sociologist Harvey Ferguson so confidently, "but this was primarily a failure to grasp what theory is, and what it is for" (2009: 42). What he says about sociology seems to apply even more to the field of general education, from which TESOL has derived its inspirations about teacher theorizing and teacher research. In its attempt to grasp what theory is, and what it is for, the TESOL profession has unintentionally created conceptual uncertainties, terminological ambiguities, and methodological anxieties about teacher theorizing and teacher research, and as a result, it has caused among many practicing teachers a widespread indifference, if not outright hostility, towards theory and theorizing.

For a long time, the TESOL profession has been sending out confusing and conflicting signals about the role of theory and theorizing. Participants in a recent symposium on "theorizing TESOL" published in *TESOL Quarterly* (Volume 42, June 2008) offer glimpses of their current thinking. Alister Cumming characterizes TESOL as an "applied field" that is concerned "primarily and pragmatically with practical activities related to the education of people learning English internationally" (p. 286). He claims that TESOL practitioners "use theories" heuristically to arrive at "theoretically-informed techniques for solving problems" (p. 289). Diane Larsen-Freeman suggests that "the role of theory in TESOL should be to increase our awareness and to encourage the quest for greater understanding, on the part of teachers and researchers" (p. 293). In his response, Julian Edge says that

> the role of theory in TESOL is to establish a notional, interim target that makes the process of theorisation credible and meaningful to those teachers who believe that their professional and personal development is well served by an ongoing, explicit commitment to increasing their awareness of why it is that they teach the way they do, along with a commitment to improving their ability to articulate that awareness, through which process of articulation the awareness itself is enhanced and augmented.
>
> *(p. 653)*

A subtle movement from application to awareness to articulation is what one can also see when it comes to teacher research and teacher theorizing. Teacher research in TESOL and also in general education has been primarily couched in terms of action research although there are variations within and across a wide spectrum. I see in the literature at least three broad strands of thought, which can be plotted on a continuum in terms of who exercises agency in teacher research. I define agency as the freedom and flexibility to initiate, execute, and evaluate classroom-based research projects.

At one end of the continuum is teacher research that is mostly controlled by the expert. The classroom teacher is considered to have neither the research skills nor the resources to independently initiate, execute, and evaluate research projects. Nevertheless, some educationists argue that teachers should be guided to do classroom-based action research so that they know why they are doing what they are doing. In this context, they make a distinction between a *professional theory* and a *personal theory* of education. A professional theory is a theory which is produced, propagated and perpetuated by experts, and it finds its way into the professional knowledge base within the professional culture. A personal theory, on the other hand, is a theory which is individually developed by teachers by testing, interpreting, and judging the usefulness of professional theories and ideas constructed by experts (O'Hanlon 1993). In this view, action research is actually theory-driven, in the sense that teachers will be researching issues that are sanctioned and guided by the established community of scholars—under their supervision, with their blessings.

This view of action research, which fits in perfectly with the knowledge transmission model of teacher education, has been severely criticized because it is seen to perpetuate a harmful, artificial dichotomy of functions between the theorist and the teacher. In other words, academic discourse becomes a medium of communication that expresses and reproduces pedagogical power (Bourdieu, Passeron & Martin 1994). As Joe Kincheloe points out:

> advocates of action research who support this teacher-as-implementor approach exhibit ideological naiveté. They are unable to recognize that the act of selecting problems for teachers to research is an ideological act, an act that trivialized the role of the teacher.
>
> *(1993: 185–86)*

Somewhere in the mid-point of the action research continuum is strand number two. It represents the attempts to combine the professional knowledge of the expert and the personal experience of the teacher. In this view, action research, according to Michael Wallace, "overlaps the areas of professional development and conventional research, and for some practicing teachers may well form a bridge between the two" (1998: 18). The relationship between the expert and the teacher is seen as a mutually enriching one because "action research can both draw on academic research (thereby providing it with a professional rationale) and also feed into it by exploring areas of professional concern" (Ibid.: 254).

The collaborative research between the researcher and the teacher stands to benefit from the theoretical knowledge-base that the researcher is considered to possess, and the practical knowledge-base the classroom teacher is expected to bring with her. In spite of the emphasis given to the role of the teacher, the whole operation remains problematic because, "within the dyad, the researcher has more power while the teacher has more knowledge" (Ulichny & Schoener 1996: 503) and therefore the teacher–researcher collaboration simply prolongs the inequality that exists between them (Stewart 2006). It has also been pointed out that, with very few exceptions, much of this kind of collaborative work is published by university researchers with single authorship, and is generally meant for professional audiences. Furthermore, if they are published with joint authorship, the researcher is invariably the first author and the teacher is invariably the second author (Crookes & Chandler 1999).

At the other end of the continuum is the third strand of teacher research that puts a premium on the agency and authority of the classroom teacher. It is based on the conviction that

> pedagogic knowledge, to be of relevance, must emerge from the practice of everyday teaching. It is the practicing teacher who is better placed to produce, understand and apply that kind of knowledge.
>
> *(Kumaravadivelu 1999b: 35)*

Undoubtedly, the main player here is the teacher, the main place is the classroom, and the expert is seen as the non-intruding mentor the teacher can rely on, whenever necessary. Evidently, this strand rejects the traditional view that "the fundamental aim of action research is to improve practice rather than to produce knowledge" (Elliot 1991: 49); instead, it reflects the view that "the thinking teacher is no longer perceived as someone who applies theories, but as someone who theorizes practice" (Edge 2001: 6). It is aimed at encouraging the teacher to consider how research in the language classroom can lead to pedagogic improvement, personal enrichment, and professional development all of which characterize the transformative model of teaching and teacher education.

A crucial question that presents itself is: what are the problems and prospects of teachers seriously doing the type of teacher research that can potentially lead them to theorize what they practice and practice what they theorize?

5.2.1 Problems and Prospects

One of the persistent problems that teachers have faced in their attempt to theorize from the classroom is that they do not get adequate actionable guidance from professional researchers in the areas of second language acquisition (SLA) and language pedagogy. Stressing the importance of SLA research, Rod Ellis (2010: 196) observes that "teachers need opportunities to become researchers in their own classroom as well as consumers of SLA research." However, "most potential consumers of SLA research are frequently repelled by its disregard for real world issues" (Markee 1997: 88, cited in Ellis 2010). A possible solution, according to Ellis, is for teachers to do collaborative research with an SLA researcher or do their own action research and exploratory practice (see below for details on exploratory practice).

Yet another problem is teachers' lack of competence and confidence in their ability to do research. Recent surveys and studies (Barkhuizen 2009, Borg 2009) show teachers' lack of knowledge of research practices as well as lack of time to do research as primary reasons. They have also reported about barriers that are attitudinal, conceptual, and procedural in nature. A related issue is that even those teachers who carry out classroom-based inquiry do not normally find avenues to share their findings with other teachers, researchers, curriculum designers, or policy makers. Not doing so "would mean missing the opportunity and ignoring the responsibility to contribute to discussions and debates in the field of language education" (Barkhuizen 2009: 124), thereby severely limiting the impact of their findings.

Research in language pedagogy has also not offered adequate support for teachers in theorizing. It is partly because, as Mark Clarke notes, the language pedagogy has narrowly pre-occupied itself with "method," shifting its focus "from improving learning to improving method, not unlike the gardener who spends an inordinate amount of time building the ideal hothouse and forgets to tend to the tomatoes" (2003: 128). Thus, methods-based teaching and teacher research have not adequately provided teachers with the knowledge and skill necessary for them to explore their own classroom in a postmethod environment where deeper engagement with the operating principles of particularity, practicality, and possibility is warranted (see Chapter 1 for details). The net result is that, although the professional literature

> is replete with persuasive arguments in favor of the benefits to teachers of being research-engaged; the reality remains though that teacher research—systematic, rigorous enquiry by teachers into their own professional contexts, and which is made public—is a minority activity in ELT.
>
> *(Borg 2009: 377)*

The real or perceived constraints not withstanding, teacher theorizing is eminently doable if properly conceived and conducted. Recent studies show that teachers have a tendency to wrongly associate teacher research with conventional forms of scientific inquiry (Borg 2007: 744). In order to dispel such a false notion, it has been suggested that teachers should be provided with

> on-going opportunities to discuss and clarify their understandings of what research is and how its worth can be judged, of the range of forms it may legitimately take, and of the ways that research and classroom practice may interact in the lives of teachers.
>
> *(Borg 2007: 744)*

In addition, we need to explicitly emphasize, as I have stated elsewhere, that teacher theorizing

> does not necessarily involve highly sophisticated, statistically laden, variable controlled experimental studies, for which practicing teachers have neither the time nor the energy. Rather, it involves keeping one's eyes, ears, and mind open in the classroom to see what works and what does not, with what group(s) of learners, and for what reason, and assessing what changes are necessary to make instruction achieve its desired goals.
>
> *(Kumaravadivelu 2001: 550)*

Of course, such a classroom observation has to be done systematically and in a sustained manner so that it will enable teachers to eventually derive a personal theory of practice (see Chapter 6).

One popular example of classroom-based inquiry is *Exploratory Practice* (EP) proposed by Dick Allwright (e.g., 2003, 2005). It is defined as "a sustainable way of developing our understanding within our practice, with the absolute minimum of intrusion, and the maximum potential for practical and personal benefit" (EP Website). The primary focus is understanding—understanding what happens in the classroom. EP involves a series of basic steps including (a) identifying a puzzle, that is, finding something puzzling in a teaching and learning situation; (b) reflecting on the puzzle, that is, thinking about the puzzle to understand it without actually taking any action; (c) monitoring, that is, paying attention to the phenomenon that is puzzling to understand it better; (d) taking direct action, that is, generating additional data from the classroom; (e) considering the outcomes reached so far, and deciding what to do next, which involves determining whether there is sufficient justification to move on or whether more reflection and more data are needed; (f) moving on, which means deciding to choose from several options to move toward transforming the current system; and (g) going public, that is, sharing the benefits of exploration with others through presentations or publications. Thus, the central focus of EP is local practice.

As the above discussion shows, certain strands of action research and the central tenets of exploratory practice have opened up a productive path for teacher theorizing. And yet, "the relationship between SLA and either action research or exploratory practice remains tenuous" (Ellis 2010: 189). This is not only because of the disjunction between the goals of acquisitional research and pedagogic theorizing but also because of methodological considerations.

5.2.2 Methodological Considerations

The conventional forms of scientific inquiry referred to above with its predominantly quantitative-oriented experimental focus is better suited for SLA researchers because they intend to use their findings to generalize, to predict, and to posit causal relationships between the phenomena they are exploring. Teacher theorizing, however, entails predominantly qualitative research involving participant observation aimed at interpretation rather than prediction (see McKay 2006 for more details). For a long time, language teaching research, like education research, was engaged in a futile exercise by following the conventional forms of scientific inquiry ignoring the lived experiences of teachers and learners. Conspicuously absent in such a focus

> are the voices of teachers, the questions and problems they pose, the frameworks they use to interpret and improve their practice, and the ways they define and understand their work lives.
>
> *(Lytle & Cochran-Smith 1990: 83)*

Luckily, the trend has been reversed somewhat in the last decade as more and more language teaching researchers opt for qualitative research methods.

In a recent state-of-the-art article, Keith Richards (2009: 149) offers a working definition of qualitative research as practiced by language teaching researchers. It is:

- locally situated (it studies human participants in natural settings and conditions, eschewing artificially constructed situations);
- participant-oriented (it is sensitive to, and seeks to understand, participants' perspectives on their world);
- holistic (it is context sensitive and does not study isolated aspects independently of the situation in which they occur);
- inductive (it depends on a process of interpretation that involves immersion in the data and draws on different perspectives).

Some of the most prominent approaches to qualitative research include case study, ethnographic analysis, and classroom interaction analysis.

Clear guidelines on qualitative research to help novice researchers have also emerged recently (see McKay 2006). The following five steps adapted from Mark Clarke (2007: 77–78) constitute a good start for beginning teacher researchers (for another set of steps, see Kumaravadivelu 2003b, Chapter 13, Monitoring Teaching Acts):

- Identify a number of classroom techniques, events, activities, or episodes that proved to be effective;
- Articulate the key elements of this successful learning/teaching experience;
- List the important attributes of the participating learners that must be attended to in order to understand the reasons behind the success;
- Identify key tenets of established learning/teaching theories that might explain and support the reasons; and
- Adopt a critical stance that permits constant revision of all the ideas in light of additional experiences, further reading and engagement with other colleagues.

Of course one can, and in fact one should, focus not just on what works in class but also on what does not work, because we can learn as much from success stories as from those that do not succeed.

Given the subjective nature of teacher research, there have been legitimate criticisms about its validity and reliability. It is important to recognize and accept that any meaning-oriented interpretive study is bound to be subjective. Care, however, must be taken to reduce subjectivity. A procedure that has been effectively used is what is called triangulation. It involves collecting multiple perspectives (see Chapter 6 for more details) using multiple data elicitation techniques (such as observations, interviews, surveys, questionnaires, etc.) and making sure the interpretations are corroborated by research partners or interested colleagues. The idea is to check whether multiple sources yield similar conclusions. It is worthwhile to keep in mind that ethnographic research, as anthropologist Clifford Geertz reminds us, is "not an experimental science in search of law but an interpretive one in search of meaning" (1973: 5).

It should be fairly clear by now that an important aspect of qualitative-oriented, ethnography-based, classroom-centered teacher research is the lived experience and the authentic voice of teachers and learners. What this essentially means is that significance is, and should be, attached more to local practice and personal experience than to professional theories of language learning and teaching. It is therefore wise to see teacher theorizing as a prolonged personal quest that gradually unveils a teacher's sense making (van Manen 1977) or a teacher's sense of plausibility (Prabhu 1990), a sustained effort that will go a long way in helping teachers theorize from the classroom. Given the interpretive character of teacher theorizing, a crucial facet of it is the creation of opportunities for the dialogic construction of meaning to take place.

5.3 Dialogizing

Teacher inquiry *is* dialogic inquiry. That is to say, the construction of even a *personal* theory of practice has to be carried out communally, collaboratively, and dialogically. What actually is dialogizing? And, why do teachers have to dialogize? Several cultural and educational theorists have provided us with penetrating thoughts on these and related matters. I consider insights from three of them vital for teacher dialoging: Mikhail Bakhtin, Etienne Wenger, and Gordon Wells.

For Bakhtin, a dialogic exchange is much more than a verbal exchange between two or more interlocutors. It is an interaction between meanings, between voices, between belief systems; an interaction that produces what Bakhtin calls, *a responsive understanding*. Bakhtinian dialogism places understanding at the core of all human endeavors. Understanding "is the culminating moment for the sake of which dialogue exists, with all elements of its complex and dynamic structure" (Marchenkova 2005: 173). Where the spirit of a truly dialogic interaction prevails, all participants learn from each other and benefit from each other regardless of hierarchical disparities in power, expertise, or experience. In a dialogic process, no one interlocutor is marginalized; no one interlocutor is privileged, for it is through dialogic relationships that interlocutors simultaneously acquire and abdicate their freedom. Therefore, the dialogic imperative carries with it the potential to shape and reshape the thought processes of both the interlocutors, resulting in reciprocal learning which eventually leads to mutual enrichment.

In *The Dialogic Imagination*, Bakhtin's translators and interpreters Carly Emerson and Michael Holquist (Bakhtin 1981) show us how his dialogism brings together seemingly disparate but powerful constructs such as history, culture, literature, language, and self-identity, and how it tries to explain the intricate relationship between human beings, between Self and society, and between Self and the Other. These relationships are shaped by a dialogic interaction that is marked by a constant tension between what Bakhtin (1981: 424) calls *authoritative discourse* and *internally-persuasive discourse*. The former

> is privileged language that approaches us from without; … We recite it. It has great power over us, but only while in power; if ever dethroned it immediately becomes a dead thing, a relic.

The latter represents "one's own words, with one's own accents, gestures, modifications" (Ibid.: 424). Human consciousness, and with it, individual identity formation,

> is a constant struggle between these two types of discourse: an attempt to assimilate more into one's own system, and the simultaneous freeing of one's own discourse from the authoritative word.
>
> *(Ibid.: 424–25)*

When the language of authoritative discourse undergoes the process of dialogization, it becomes de-privileged. Undialogized language remains "authoritative or absolute" (Ibid.: 427). With certain limits, one can draw a useful analogy between the construction of authoritative discourse and internally-persuasive discourse, and the construction of the expert's professional knowledge and the teacher's personal knowledge (more on this later).

Clearly, individuals play a paramount agentive role in the process of dialogization but not without the active participation from the social or professional communities that they are part of. This is where the notion of community of practice becomes relevant. A community of practice refers to a group of people who are bound together by a commonly-shared concern or a passion for something, and regularly interact with each other in order to deepen their knowledge, sharpen their skills, and enrich their experience (Lave & Wenger 1991). Community of practice is comprehensive theory that encompasses different traditions of situated learning, identity formation, and construction of meaning, and explores in a comprehensive manner how "the production, transformation, and change in the identities of persons, knowledgeable skill in practice, and communities of practice are realized in the lived-in world of engagement in everyday activity" (p. 41).

Expanding on the earlier Lave and Wenger work, Wenger (1998) defines a community of practice along three dimensions:

- What it is about—its *joint enterprise* as understood and continually renegotiated by its members;
- How it functions—mutual engagement that bind members together into a social entity; and
- What capability it has produced—the *shared repertoire* of communal resources (routines, sensibilities, artifacts, vocabulary, styles, etc.) that members have developed over time.

A central characteristic of community of practice is that it is the community, not any external force, that produces the practice and thus a community of practice functions as a fundamentally self-organizing and self-monitoring system.

As Wenger rightly points out, we all belong to a number of communities of practice—at work, at school, at home, at a club, at a place of worship, and more. As members of these communities of practice, we gain different experiences and develop multiple identities. As we glide from one community of practice to another, we encounter boundaries of practice. Our "practice" in one community (say, a club) may be different from our "practice" in another (say, a place of worship). Our multimembership demands reconciliation with various boundaries of practice. As a result, we try to engage our whole person in practice in order to creatively and dynamically negotiate our own activities, identities, and relations. "The creative negotiation of an identity," Wenger observes,

> always has the potential to rearrange these relations. In this regard multimembership is not just a matter of personal identity. The work of reconciliation is a profoundly social kind of work.
>
> *(1998: 161)*

And, this kind of work demands that we engage in dialogic interaction with other members of our communities of practice. As we "interact with each other and with the world, we tune our relations with each other and with the world accordingly. In other words we learn" (Ibid.: 45).

Expanding on Wenger's idea of communities of practice, and combining it with Bakhtin's dialogism, Wells (1999) calls for *communities of inquiry*. A community of inquiry is a particular type of community of practice that applies specifically to teachers. His central argument is that "education should be conducted as a dialogue about matters of interest and concern to the participants" (p. xi). He does not see inquiry, as it is normally seen in educational circles, as a method (as in "discovery" learning) nor as a ready-made set of generic procedures for carrying out certain classroom activities. Instead, he sees it as

> a stance toward experiences and ideas − a willingness to wonder, to ask questions, to seek to understand by collaborating with others in the attempt to make answers to them.
>
> *(Ibid.: 121)*

The aim of such an inquiry is not knowing-for-the-sake-of-knowing, but learning to develop the disposition and ability necessary "to act informedly and responsibly in the situations that may be encountered both now and in the future" (Ibid.: 121). Furthermore, such an inquiry should help teachers build upon the lived experiences of their learners and encourage them "to be agentive in directing their own learning" and "equip them with the socially valued ways of thinking and acting ... " (Ibid.: 121).

Wells believes that teachers' community of inquiry is different from other communities of practice because it has the potential to become a community of knowledge builders. One of its distinguishing features is the importance it attaches to *metaknowing,* which gives its members the capacity to think *about* knowledge building and *about* the tools and practices involved in the process. The development of theoretical knowing occurs when teachers draw on relevant first-hand experiences and "engage in the discourse of knowledge building in order to make connections among the different objects and activities with which they are involved" (Ibid.: 124) and, in doing so, they develop "systematic conceptual structures" that constitute knowledge. Working collaboratively with others on questions and problems that arise from their classroom practice, members of the teaching community create "a framework within which individual development and societal transformation are achieved" (Ibid.: 122).

To sum up, what we learn from the three theorists is that a truly dialogic interaction between participants can lead to a responsive understanding of one another's beliefs, identities and dispositions, which in turn can lead to personal and professional growth. The interlocutors function as members of a community of practice and work collaboratively to enhance their knowledge, and enrich their experience. Teachers, in particular, constitute communities of inquiry engaging in knowledge production in addition to performing their familiar role in knowledge dissemination. All three theorists, in one way or another, focus on

> the intentional activity of individuals who, as members of a community, make use of and produce representations in the collaborative attempt to better understand and transform their shared world.
>
> *(Wells 1999: 76)*

These thoughts have immense value for helping teachers dialogize.

5.3.1 Teacher Dialogizing

Simply put, teacher dialogizing is about having conversations with Self, with texts and with others on matters related to learning, teaching, and theorizing. The conversation, however, must be constant, continual, and critical. It must also be *a learning conversation*. Working in the field of business management learning, Chris Argyris (1992) distinguishes between *controlling conversations* and *learning conversations*. The former, as the name suggests, is about imposing one's own views on others with the view to controlling the conversation and the ensuing conduct regardless of merits. The latter is about treating diversity of views as a resource for learning, for questioning one's own beliefs, assumptions, and values. The ideal conversation between participants in a dialogic inquiry should be a learning conversation in which "different points of view are respected and treated as a resource for reciprocal critique and learning" (Argyris 1992: 53).

The teacher as dialogic inquirer engaged in learning conversations with peers and mentors should be able to figure out different conversational opportunities that may carry different values. In a study that explored the process and content of mentors' professional conversations as opportunities for collaboratively constructing knowledge, Lily Orland-Barak (2006) has identified three different forms of dialogues that operated complementarily in the conversations: convergent, divergent and parallel dialogues. In convergent dialogues, participants mediate understandings leading to convergence of learning opportunities that provide solutions to a problem brought to the conversational floor. In divergent dialogues, participants depart from their personal contexts in order to explore, compare and make connections across various practices in order to engage in broader and more generalized aspects of theorizing. In parallel dialogues, participants use the conversational space as a setting for developing their own ideas in a kind of conversation with Self. These dialogues present themselves alternately in a single conversation, with one or the other form prevailing at any given time. They provide "important opportunities for participants to discriminate and dispute their own ideologies and fixed assumptions" (p. 20).

In order to dispute their own fixed assumptions, student teachers, practicing teachers and cooperating teachers often look for learning conversational opportunities that will yield new experiences, new interpretations, and new evaluations. In a study on the use of collaborative dialogue between cooperating teachers and student teachers, Derin Atay (2004) reported what the participants learned from learning conversations. One cooperating teacher said "Having to discuss my teaching practices in such detail with someone over a long period of time, caused me to delve into my own practices and change some of them" (p. 153). Another said that working with a student teacher

> prompted him to think about and subsequently articulate the theoretical knowledge behind his teaching practice and he commented that "once you start explaining and sharing your ideas you realize what you are carrying in your head."

(Ibid.: 154)

Some of the case studies from the field of TESOL (for example, Richards ed. 1998, Edge ed. 2001) present interesting stories in which teachers and teacher educators share episodes of their learning conversations using their narrative and autobiographical voice.

Autobiographical narrative is a valuable device teachers can effectively use as part of their dialogic inquiry. It offers "insights into people's private worlds" (Pavlenko 2007: 164). The absorbing narrative stories included in the volume edited by Karen Johnson and Paula Golombek (2002) reveal how, using narrative inquiry as systematic exploration, teachers are able to "recall, rethink, and reconstruct their own ways of knowing" (p. xi) and how teacher theorizing is not a linear but "a dynamic interplay between description, reflection, dialogue with self and others, and the implementation of alternative teaching practices" (Ibid.: 7).

One narrative story talks about how a teacher successfully creates an avenue of communication between the students and herself, and discovers that maximizing learning opportunities in class is

> as simple as making a connection between ourselves and our students in a truly human way, in a way that says, I know this is hard work, let's do the work together, let's learn together, let's muck about in the messy place of learning together.
>
> *(Ibid.: 32)*

Another recalls the art of drawing theory from the classroom, and based on personal experiences offers recommendations for others:

> Write an autobiography in which you capture the richness of your experiences and beliefs as a student, language learner, and language teacher. Identify important people or critical incidents that significantly influenced your understandings of your professional development as a language teacher. Then, critically analyze those experiences and beliefs in terms of how they have shaped you as a teacher and a learner of teaching. Finally, apply the resulting insights you gained to your current or future teaching practices.
>
> *(Ibid.: 175)*

5.4 In Closing

As the above quoted teacher recommendation indicates, the doing of teaching, theorizing, and dialogizing are all closely intertwined. They nurture each other in an ever evolving cycle of formation and transformation. Teaching is a reflective activity which at once shapes and is shaped by the doing of theorizing which in turn is bolstered by the collaborative process of dialogic inquiry. In this chapter, I focused on how the doing of teaching in the language classroom is marked by efforts to maximize learning opportunities and to mentor personal transformation. I then discussed the type of teacher research that can potentially lead teachers to theorize what they practice and practice what they theorize. Finally, I touched upon how the construction of even a personal theory of practice has to be carried out collabora- tively and dialogically. All along, running like an undercurrent, is a call for developing a transformative model of teacher education that can equip the teachers with the knowledge, skill, and disposition necessary to become transformative intellectuals.

In carrying out the doing of teaching, theorizing, and dialogizing, teachers develop what Hansen (2001) calls *tenacious humility*—"an active quality of staying the course while respecting reality"—a quality that creates "conditions for teacher learning, for a 'deeper knowledge' of the 'necessities' entailed in 'good practice'" (p. 172). The necessities entailed in good practice also entail *seeing* the events and activities of the classroom from multiple perspectives. We turn to that subject next.

Rapid Reader Response

Write a quick response to the following questions. Form small groups, share your thoughts and discuss them with other members of the group.

1   What is the one big point you learned from this chapter?
2   What is the one main unanswered question you leave the chapter with?
3   What is the one surprising idea or concept you encountered in this chapter?
4   What is one example of terminology or concept you did not fully understand?

Reflective Tasks

Task 5.1 Creating Learning Opportunities

T.5.1.1 Do you agree with the statement that the quality of learning opportunity created in the classroom is closely related to whether teachers see their roles as passive technicians, reflective practitioners, or transformative intellectuals?

T.5.1.2 In what way, do you think, the quality of learning opportunities is linked to teacher roles? Give specific examples.

T.5.1.3 Which of the three teacher roles is best suited to create high quality learn- ing opportunities in class, and why?

T.5.1.4 Recall any recent classroom episode that you may have experienced as a student teacher or as a practicing teacher, and think about the reasons why it did or did not create high quality learning opportunities.

T.5.1.5 Is there anything that learners can (or should) do to facilitate the creation of high quality learning opportunities in class?

Task 5.2 Doing Action Research

T.5.2.1 In the context of action research, I presented three strands of thought which can be plotted on a continuum in terms of who exercises agency. Read the relevant section again.

T.5.2.2 Which one of the strands appeals to you most and why?

T.5.2.3 What support and resources do you need if you wish to do action research following the strand that appeals to you?

T.5.2.4 What constraints (institutional, societal, cultural, etc.) do you think will hinder your attempt to do your own action research?

T.5.2.5 What are the ways in which you can overcome those constraints?

Task 5.3 Having Learning Conversations

T.5.3.1 We learned that teacher dialogizing is about having conversations with Self, with texts, and with others. However, it must also be *a learning conversation*.

T.5.3.2 What does *learning conversation* mean to you in your specific learning/ teaching context?

T.5.3.3 Describe a learning conversation you recently had with yourself on a matter related to classroom learning or teaching.

T.5.3.4 Describe a learning conversation you recently had with a classmate (or a colleague) of yours on a matter related to classroom learning or teaching.

T.5.3.5 What did you learn from these conversations (with Self, and with your partner) and how did it impact on your learning/teaching activity?

Exploratory Projects

Project 5.1 Thinking Teacher

P.5.1.1 This project is aimed at helping you to think about a "thinking teacher." Recall the statement by Julian Edge (2001: 6): "The thinking teacher is no longer perceived as someone who applies theories, but as someone who theorizes practice." Try to form a small group (with classmates or colleagues). First respond to the following questions individually and then share your views with other members of the group. Discuss the reasons behind different perspectives that may emerge.

P.5.1.2 Who, in your view, is a "thinking teacher"? What characteristics/roles do you associate with a "thinking teacher"?

P.5.1.3 What have you learned during your teacher education program that you think will help you (or has helped you) to become a "thinking teacher"?

P.5.1.4 What do you think is the difference between applying theory and theorizing practice? Give specific examples drawn from your personal experience, where possible.

P.5.1.5 Select any one well-articulated theory that you learned during your teacher education program (whether it is from the field of second language acquisition or language pedagogy), and show how it has shaped, in a cogent and connected way, your thinking about language, language learning, and language teaching.

Project 5.2 Theorizing Teacher

P.5.2.1 This project is designed to prompt you to construct a personal theory on a specific pedagogic practice. Read this quote from Rod Ellis carefully: "The acquisition of grammatical system of an L2 is a complex process and almost certainly can be assisted best by a variety of approaches. But what is important is to recognize what options are available, what the theoretical rationales for these options are, and what the problems are with these rationales. This is the starting point for developing a personal theory of grammar teaching" (2006: 103).

Try to form a small group (with classmates or colleagues). First respond to the following questions individually and then share your views with other members of the group. Discuss the reasons behind different perspectives that may emerge. In order to have a focused discussion and to facilitate useful comparisons, I suggest that all of you choose the article system of English. You choose the context (ESL, EFL, or adult education) and the proficiency level (beginning, intermediate, or advanced) of your learners.

P.5.2.2 Briefly describe all the options (in terms of "approaches") that are available for teaching the article system.

P.5.2.3 Choose any two "approaches" that you are familiar with and describe their theoretical rationale.

P.5.2.4 Discuss the "problems" with the rationales governing the two "approaches" you selected.

P.5.2.5 Considering the approaches, rationales and problems that you describe above, construct your "personal theory of grammar teaching" with specific reference to the article system. Illustrate your "personal theory" by presenting a lesson plan for teaching the article system. Make sure your plan delineates, with appropriate examples, various steps of classroom technique you will follow in your class.

6

SEEING

The question is not what you look at, but what you see.

(Henry David Thoreau, Journal, 5 August 1851)

6.0 Introduction

Seeing is like a thread that interlaces the tapestry of all the teacher preparation modules—knowing, analyzing, recognizing, and doing—we have explored so far. Its role is sometimes hidden, sometimes visible but it is always present. And yet, seeing has seldom received the kind of attention it deserves and demands, particularly in the field of education and TESOL. In this chapter, I will first provide necessary background information about the concept of seeing, and its connection to the language classroom. Then, I will discuss the importance of critical classroom observation, highlighting the need for seeing the teacher, learner, and observer perspectives through self as well as peer observation. We will see how seeing is connected to teachers' professional development and why teacher education programs should pay greater attention to it.

For understanding the concept of seeing in the context of learning and teaching, I turn to Tone Kvernbekk, an educationist from Norway. Kvernbekk (2000) brings a philosophical outlook to the complexities and dimensions of the concept of seeing. He first narrates the traditional view of seeing that is prevalent in educational circles. As he points out, the traditional wisdom holds that people simply see the things that are conventionally "there" and that is also something which everybody else sees. Furthermore, they trust what they see. This kind of seeing is based mostly on familiarity, experience, and commonsense. It is embedded in human propensity. It therefore requires extraordinary capacity to stop seeing the things that are conventionally "there" to be seen.

This commonsense view also holds that what teachers and student teachers normally gain by observation, by what they see, is not scientific knowledge but rather perceptual knowledge. This is because this kind of seeing is *simple seeing* (later dubbed as *seeing-in*) and it merely involves superficially looking at objects as they appear, without critical engagement. Kvernbekk disagrees with this view somewhat because, for him, it "implies that what a teacher can see is restricted to directly observable objects or directly perceptible properties of objects … " (2000: 368). He thinks that "we see a lot more than this; we also see events, states of affairs and facts" (Ibid.: 368) and that "direct and indirect fact perception probably accounts for the vast majority of perceptions professionals make in practice" (Ibid.: 369).

Critically responding to, and conceptually expanding, what he finds in the education literature, Kvernbekk talks about two other forms of seeing: *seeing-as*, and *seeing-that*. Without going deep into his philosophical discourse, *seeing-as* can be described as an attempt to make sense of the experience of current observation by identifying similarities and dissimilarities between past experiences, images, and actions, and the new ones. Thus, *seeing-as* goes beyond immediate sensory perception. In explaining his views, Kvernbekk invokes the views of yet another educationist, Donald Schön (1983) whose statement he endorses:

> It is our capacity to see unfamiliar situations as familiar ones, and to do in the former as we have done in the latter, that enables us to bring our past experience to bear on the unique case. It is our capacity to *see-as* and *do-as* that allows us to have a feel for problems that do not fit existing rules.
>
> *(Schön 1983, original emphasis, cited in Kvernbekk 2000: 361)*

Seeing-that is a higher form of seeing that involves critical application of knowledge and therefore it "is an epistemic achievement" (Ibid.: 362). It is seen as a tool for expressing the relationship between seeing and knowing. In other words, it is critically mediated by seeing and knowing thus forging new connections between the conceptual and the perceptual. Demanding a critical interpretation of what we see, it opens up avenues for seeing objects and properties of objects as more than what appears on the surface. Kvernbekk cautions us saying that the education literature contains instances of many student teachers and teachers merely seeing objects and properties of objects but falsely expressing them in terms of *seeing-that*. He says:

> One sees *that* a student is writing, *that* two students make a drawing together and *that* the classroom floor has not been washed. And one cannot recognize that the student is writing unless one knows what it *is* to write.
>
> *(Ibid.: 365, original emphasis)*

Kvernbekk's concerns about superficial forms of seeing practiced in educational circles are real. Using his framework for seeing, Lily Orland-Barak and Shosh Leshem (2009) conducted a study in the context of a teacher education program, focusing on the nature and the impact of classroom observations as revealed in the year-long portfolios student teachers maintained. They concluded that student teachers' remarks raise "serious questions about the impact of observation on prospective teachers' sense making of their teaching experience" even though student teachers provided "illustrative cases of 'seeing as,' 'seeing in,' and 'seeing that'" (p. 31). Their findings "suggest the need to help students to make connections between the different forms of seeing, in an effort to conceptualize experience at higher levels of 'seeing that'" (Ibid.: 33). If student teachers and practicing teachers are struggling to make the connection between the different forms of seeing, it is probably because most teacher education programs do not adequately make the connection between the different forms of seeing and classroom observation.

The significance of understanding the classroom actors and activities can hardly be overstated. As Earl Stevick (1980: 4) points out, success in the classroom "depends less on materials, techniques and linguistic analyses, and more on what goes on inside and between people in the classroom." Therefore, the task of seeing what happens there becomes paramount. I have discussed elsewhere three different approaches to classroom observation: interaction approach, discourse approach, and critical approach (Kumaravadivelu 1999a). By the way, it is not at all a conceptual stretch to link, in broad and overlapping terms, the three observational approaches to the three forms of seeing discussed above. It makes sense to treat the interaction approach as producing mostly *seeing-in*, the discourse approach as prompting mostly *seeing-as*, and the critical approach as promoting mostly *seeing-that*.

To put it briefly, the interaction approach favors the use of preselected and predetermined categories for describing talk in the classroom, emphasizing the observer perception of observable behavior, giving little consideration to classroom processes or to learning outcomes. The result, as happens in the *seeing-in* form of observation, is a superficial understanding of classroom acts and activities, objects, and properties of objects. The discourse approach attempts to make sense of classroom discourse by taking into consideration turn-taking patterns, topic selection and treatment, and managerial and cognitive aspects of classroom tasks. The result, as happens in the *seeing-as* form of observation, is a fairly good understanding of the connection between past and current classroom experiences. The critical approach recognizes the complex and competing world of discourses that exist in the classroom, thereby enabling teachers to reflect on and cope with sociocultural and sociopolitical structures that directly or indirectly shape the character and content of classroom discourse. The result, as happens in the *seeing-that* form of observation, is a deeper understanding of the relationship between seeing and knowing, a relationship that can open up personal and pedagogic possibilities.

A deeper understanding of the sociocultural and sociopolitical aspects of classroom discourse, and the ability to do *seeing-that* form of observation and analysis can emerge only by following a critical approach to classroom observation. In this regard, the principles and practices of critical classroom discourse analysis (CCDA) offer a productive pathway (Kumaravadivelu 1999a: 472). CCDA is based on the premise that the lived experiences learners and teachers bring with them to the classroom setting "are motivated and molded not just by the learning and teaching episodes they encounter in the classroom but also by the broader linguistic, social, economic, political, and historical milieu in which they all grow up." What this means is that the aim of classroom observation should not be limited, as has generally been the case, to an analysis of teacher input and learner output, the Initiation-Response-Feedback (IRF) sequence and all its variations, or the teaching strategies followed by the teacher; instead, it "should also take into account discourse participants' complex and competing expectations and beliefs, identities and voices, and fears and anxieties" (Ibid.: 472). This view has been strengthened by more recent studies (e.g., Richards 2006, Walsh 2006) that address "the dynamic nature of identity construction and its relationship to the development of ongoing talk" in the language classroom (Richards 2006: 51).

Because expectations, beliefs, identities, voices, fears, and anxieties vary enormously among participants, how they see classroom actors and activities will also vary. Therefore, any meaningful attempt to see what happens in the classroom must take into consideration different perspectives learners, teachers, and observers bring to the classroom, and the perceptions they develop about their classroom experience.

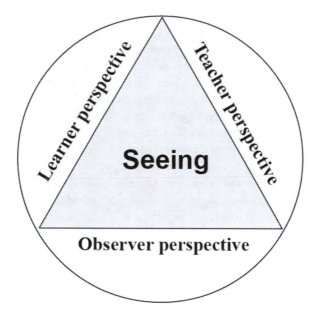

6.1 Learner Perspective

The emphasis on the learner perspective recognizes that, as interested and involved members of the classroom community, learners are best suited to explain and examine several aspects of classroom life that pertain to them, including the stated or unstated objectives of classroom activities, the clarity of instructional guidance given by the teacher to help them achieve those objectives, the articulated or unarticulated modes of on-going self-evaluation they use to monitor and assess the progress they are making in carrying out the activity at hand, and their overall attitude toward the nature and scope of classroom events and activities. Given the complex role learners play, it is not easy to see classroom talk from the learners' perspective. Part of the challenge lies in the fact that classroom talk, as Michael Breen tells us:

> has meaning potential that is layered in being both superficially immediate and traceable to an explicit topic or content yet also always framed *intra-personally* within both the conscious and unconscious learning agenda of the individual learners and framed *interpersonally* within the discourse of the language classroom. The former is, of course, less accessible to the researcher. The latter, however, may be more accessible and, therefore, a medium through which we may better understand both the process and outcomes of learner participation.
>
> *(2001: 129, original emphasis)*

The fact that the intrapersonal nature of learner participation is largely inaccessible for empirical verification has not deterred SLA researchers from metaphorically constructing profiles of L2 learners. Rod Ellis (2001) has compiled basic metaphors used by nine prominent SLA researchers. These metaphors can and do shape our expectations about the role learners might play in jointly producing classroom discourse. They may also shape what learners do in the classroom, and how they and others see what they do. Here are some choice metaphors (pp. 72–85):

- *Learner as container:* According to this metaphor, learners are seen as passive and restricted. Passive because they have things done to them rather than do things themselves. Restricted because they have limited capacities for learning, both in the sense of what they can notice and what they can remember;
- *Learner as machine:* According to this metaphor, learners lack control over what they do to learn and how they do it. Researchers and teachers determine what goes into the machine (input), what comes out of it (output), and how to manipulate the two (what ecological conditions must prevail and be modified for the machine to work);
- *Learner as negotiator:* According to this metaphor, learners undertake delicate negotiations with themselves and others to determine what is good for them. This metaphor puts the learners in a much more active and agentive role than the two previous ones;
- *Learner as problem-solver:* According to this metaphor, learners act like a scientific investigator who forms, tests, and confirms/rejects hypotheses. They are

cognitively active in shaping what they learn and how they learn it. Ellis thinks that by using this common metaphor, "researchers are perhaps creating learners in their own image. Just as they seek to solve problems *about* learning so learners solve problems *in order to* learn" (Ibid.: 75, original emphasis);

- *Learner as builder.* According to this metaphor, learners construct and restructure their interlanguages. Using all the "scaffolding" provided by teachers and text-books, learners construct metalinguistic understanding of grammatical rules and other units of language as system;
- *Learner as investor.* According to this metaphor, learners draw from their linguistic and cultural capital and make an affective investment in order get the maximum gain out of their classroom enterprise;
- *Learner as struggler.* According to this metaphor, learners find their classrooms as sites of struggle. They must be prepared to show resistance to inequitable social, cultural and political forces that try to keep them from personal transformation.

There is a multitude of other metaphors, "some quite idiosyncractic" (Ibid.: 77). However, most of them, according to Ellis, characterize the learners as agents in their own learning. There are indeed differences among researchers, and between researchers and learners about these profiles but "differences may not matter" because "researchers and learners have different agendas—learners to learn and researchers to describe and explain learning" (Ibid.: 84).

Differences, however, do matter when it comes to seeing learner perspectives because "the more we know about the learner's personal approaches and personal concepts, the better and more productive our intervention will be" (Kumaravadivelu 1991: 107). A recent study of learner perceptions of classroom interaction, particularly learner-learner interaction, exposes acutely differing perceptions about issues of communicative intelligibility, grammatical accuracy, and corrective feedback (Kuo 2011). Another study on learner perception of learning objectives in an EFL context reveals that the learners could not correctly identify the teacher's learning objectives and that there exists a huge gap between what the teacher actually did and how differently the learners see them (Wong 2009). Yet another study in which teachers and learners evaluated course tasks together shows a multiplicity of perspectives, along with the benefits of collaborative evaluation and reflection (Stewart 2007). An earlier project involving 997 learners and 50 teachers of English examined the degree of correspondence between learners' preferred activities and the activities teachers believed the learners liked. The researcher found only 50 per cent correspondence between them (Spratt 1999).

The perception gaps are as glaring as they are common (Kumaravadivelu 1991, Block 1994, Barkhuizen 1998). A possible remedy is first to identify the sources of perceptual mismatches and then try to reduce them. One can identify at least ten potential sources of mismatch between teacher intention and learner interpretation: cognitive (knowledge of the world); communicative (skills needed to exchange messages); linguistic (knowledge of the still developing target language); pedagogic (recognition of teaching objectives); strategic (awareness of learning strategies and styles); cultural (knowledge of the target cultural norms); evaluative (self-evaluation measures used by learners to monitor progress); procedural (tactics needed to resolve a specific problem); instructional (directions given by teachers to help learners perform tasks); and attitudinal (participants' disposition towards the nature of learning, teaching, and role relationships) (see Kumaravadivelu 1991, 2003b for illustrative examples).

Given the nature of communication in the language classroom, mismatches may be unavoidable, but they are remediable. One way of closing the gap in perceptions is "to build into our lessons more time to explain, discuss and evaluate activities and approaches" (Spratt 1999: 149). Other suggestions (Barkhuizen 1998) include asking the learners (a) to keep journal entries about how they see what happens in the classroom; (b) to write letters to their teachers about teaching and the learning opportunities created or missed; (c) to write compositions about their language learning experiences; (d) to listen for suggestions from other learners; (e) to give their teachers detailed feedback on tests and other assignments; and (f) to take teacher-administered course evaluations both during and at the end of a term.

Recognizing and reducing perceptual mismatches will help us see learner perspectives in a new and productive light. If we are serious about pursuing *seeing-that* as a preferable form of classroom observation, then, "we are obliged to hear the multiplicity of meanings *given* to what is done by the people who undertake teaching and learning together" (Breen 1991: 232, original emphasis). Clearly, the multiplicity of meanings we hear from the classroom emanates not just from the learner but from the teacher as well. Therefore, seeing the teacher perspective becomes equally crucial.

6.2 Teacher Perspective

Even though the multiplicity of meanings emanating from the classroom is the result of joint endeavors by learners and teachers, there is no gainsaying the fact that what is involved is essentially an asymmetrical relationship. There is asymmetry in the knowledge-base as well as in the power-base. It is the teacher who plans and conducts the lesson, selects and modifies text materials, and adopts and adapts teaching methods. It is the teacher who most often drives the engine that starts, steers, and stops the classroom talk. It is the teacher who decides whether to abdicate the authority vested in her, and to what extent. It is the teacher who is best suited to describe the thinking behind her decisions and actions. It then follows that understanding the teacher perspective is essential for understanding the nature of classroom learning and teaching.

In the previous section on learner perspective, we learned about metaphorical representations of learner roles from an essay by Rod Ellis. A recent study by Thomas Farrell (2011) presents similar representations of teacher roles, with one crucial difference. Ellis' work is a compilation of ideas from nine prominent SLA scholars whereas Ferrell's is a contribution from qualitative research involving three experienced, native-speaking Canadian teachers of English as a second language. In this study, the teachers themselves reflect on their work and recount their professional identities. Based on the data, Ferrell identifies a total of sixteen sub-identities and divides them into three major role identity clusters: teacher as manager, teacher as acculturator, and teacher as professional.

Teacher as manager attempts to manage and control everything that happens in the classroom. This cluster includes three frequently mentioned sub-identities: teacher as vendor, seen as a seller of institutional interests and also of a particular teaching method; teacher as entertainer, seen as a teller of jokes and stories; and teacher as communication controller, seen as one who controls classroom interaction dynamics (turn taking, turn giving, etc). Teacher as acculturator is about engaging in activities that help learners become accustomed to the cultural beliefs and practices of the target language community. This cluster includes the two most frequently occurring sub-identities: teacher as socializer, seen as one who gets involved in extracurricular, socializing activities with students; and teacher as social worker, seen as one who offers advice to students just like a social worker does. Teacher as professional relates to carrying out duties with a sense of professionalism. This cluster includes the most frequently occurring sub-identity: teacher as collaborator who willingly and seriously works and shares professional knowledge with other teachers, and gives advice to other ESL teachers. Rightly presenting these teacher profiles as provisional rather than definitive, Farrell contends that these representations will help teachers "become more aware of their role identity and then decide if and how they may want to make changes to their roles" (Farrell 2011: 61). Besides, these representations, as was stated about learner profiles, may be treated as factors that could shape what work teachers do, and how they see their work.

In addition to the above mentioned self-perceived teacher identity roles, what will also be of help in seeing the teacher perspective is the teacher's view of what constitutes a good language class. A comprehensive study conducted by Rose Senior offers useful insights. Her findings are unambiguous:

> in the minds of teachers, good classes were those that functioned effectively as groups. The notion of class cohesiveness was therefore the central phenomenon, or core category, to which all other categories could be linked.
>
> *(2006: 5)*

In creating and maintaining class cohesiveness, teachers try to

> ensure that the social atmosphere of the classroom is neither too serious nor too light-hearted, neither too heavy nor too frothy – sensing that a balance between these two extremes is desirable.
>
> *(Ibid.: 272)*

Teachers are willing and able to make suitable adjustments in their teaching agenda in order to promote social harmony in class. These adjustments include looking intently for ongoing student feedback, based on which they deviate regularly from what they intended to teach. In practical terms, these adjustments most often take the form of not slavishly sticking to lesson plans, and not strictly following the prescribed textbooks.

Teachers also engage in self-critical evaluation which reveals how sensitive they are to learner needs, motivation, and autonomy (see Chapter 4). Any teacher self-evaluation based on observation in the classroom, "is of considerable value as a process of consciousness raising and enhancing understanding" (Walsh 2006: 127). It is the raised consciousness that we see in a teacher who, recognizing and reflecting on the huge amount of class time taken up by her own talk, says after listening to her recorded voice: "there was quite a lot of 'extended teacher turn' maybe too much you know when I was listening to it perhaps there were one or two occasions when I needn't have used it" (reported in Walsh 2006: 128). Yet another teacher chides herself for her habit of using too much "everyday talk" in the class, and reflects on her

> engrained habits that I would have to take a crow-bar to prise out of myself. Or maybe wouldn't want to remove, but maybe it's a good idea to be aware of them, that they can take over or that they can sometimes not be the most constructive approach.
>
> *(reported in Walsh 2006: 139)*

It is the same raised consciousness that we see in another teacher who spends a substantial amount of time trying to gather information about the learners' backgrounds and opinions because

> without this knowledge, I would be operating in the dark; I would be giving information to students without being able to predict its effect or effectiveness. I did not need the students' personal histories, their private feelings, or information they were not comfortable sharing, but I could not teach well without drawing out of them the reasons behind their comfort or discomfort with our work.
>
> *(reported in Johnson & Golombek 2002: 84)*

In their attempt to exercise self-critical evaluation, teachers seek and benefit from comments and suggestions from outside observers as well.

6.3 Observer Perspective

A purposeful and periodical dialogue with an observing and observant person gives an opportunity for teachers to examine their pedagogic principles and practices. Getting the observer perspective on classroom events and activities can produce valuable and valued insights for them to see their work in a new and critical light.

Depending on the context and purpose, outside observers may be teacher educators, master teachers, cooperating teachers, supervisors, or peers. Teachers can avail the opportunity for getting outsider perspectives at two phases in their professional development: through teaching practice during their days as student teachers, and through peer evaluation during their days as practicing teachers. A notable limitation in discussing the observer perspective is that there is very little in the professional literature on education and TESOL that provides first hand information about what observers do in pre-service and in-service contexts. We can, however, make some gainful inferences from what has been reported by learners as well as student teachers.

It is fair to assume that some of the perceptions teachers have about teacher identities, roles, and responsibilities begin to be shaped during the days of their practicum (aka teaching practice or practice teaching) as part of their teacher education program. Practicum, which is a core course in most TESOL teacher education programs, generally deals with issues such as lesson plans, classroom communication, classroom management, and rapport with master teachers, cooperating teachers, and others (see Crookes 2003 for more details). The most common feature of the course is classroom observation, in which student teachers not only go and observe their master teacher or cooperating teacher teach but also have their own practice teaching observed. In many instances, they also observe their classmates as part of the microteaching practices involving the teaching of a short 5–10 minute micro-lesson with a very specific and narrow focus, followed by feedback from the teacher educator and fellow student teachers.

The observers—teacher educators, master teachers, or cooperating teachers—bear a heavy burden in observing the teaching of student teachers. Crucially, they have to make a distinction between observation for class assessment and observation for professional development—a distinction that is subtle and difficult to make. Observation for class assessment is usually "value-based, directive, externally imposed, and colored by factors not necessarily related to learning, it does not fall within our central notion of observation as a learning tool" (Wajnryb 1992: 2). Observation for professional development is about guiding student teachers, as John Fanselow (1990) would say, in their journey towards discovery and self-knowledge. Observers are faced with the task of providing student teachers with a learning experience that is meaningful, rewarding, and non-threatening.

One of the challenges in creating a meaningful, rewarding, and non-threatening learning experience through classroom observation is that student teachers come to their teaching practice having undergone *an apprenticeship of observation*—the idea that student teachers, even before they begin their teacher education program, may have already observed nearly 13,000 hours of teaching during their schooling (Lortie 1975). By virtue of that apprenticeship, they bring with them firmly entrenched images of what teaching is all about. Added to the mix are the new and sometimes conflicting insights they gain during their teacher education programs. As a result, they develop a nagging skepticism about the use of observed teaching practice.

Research in TESOL teacher preparation reveals how student teachers deal with potential tensions that may arise owing to certain principles and practices advocated by their teacher educator, master teacher, or co-operating teacher (Brandt 2007, Farrell 2008). For instance, it is reported that student teachers feel that they are often compelled to perform according to the expectations and preferences of their teacher educators, and that they had insufficient opportunities in which to experiment with newly learned ideas and make mistakes without being judged. One student teacher commented: "I was never comfortable with ritualized techniques for drilling and eliciting, nor with the use of flashcards in any form. Some of these things had, for me, an element of a 'performing monkey' to them" (reported in Brandt 2007: 358). It is also reported that some cooperating teachers (CTs):

> strongly encouraged the learner teachers to "rigidly follow" their way of teaching and that they felt pressure to conform to the CTs' way because after all, the CTs would be evaluating them at the end of the practicum.
>
> *(reported in Farrell 2008: 234–35)*

Some of the reported tensions arise in part because of the inherent conflict between the objectives of observation for class assessment and the objectives of observation for professional development. These tensions dissipate when student teachers complete their teacher preparation program and start teaching, which gives them the opportunity to gain from observer perspectives through peer observation done on a voluntary basis. In fact, both the observer and the observed can reap mutual benefits when "observation becomes not a vehicle for the judgment of others on the basis of our own assumptions, but instead an assessment of those assumptions on the basis of their teaching" (Cosh 1999: 27).

Research suggests that practicing teachers do find peer observation beneficial and are willing to participate if certain conditions exist (Crookes 2003). There are several practical constraints that have to be overcome. Teachers have to find peer observers who are willing to invest their time into observing and critiquing their lessons, and also willing and able to provide honest feedback pointing to things that really need to be addressed (Cosh 1999). If observers feel uncomfortable giving constructive criticism and focus only on the positive points in a lesson, "the whole exercise becomes a pointless act of mutual backpatting" (Cosh 1999: 24). In this context, there is an imperative need to work towards developing mutual trust, and one way of doing that is to openly talk about it right at the outset, and by committing to keeping the contents of any meeting or report confidential (Farrell 2008).

In spite of the constraints involved, peer observation offers opportunities for practicing teachers to monitor and evaluate their own teaching acts with the help of their colleagues. Working together as a team in a collaborative and consultative spirit, teachers strive to become joint explorers in the language classroom. The main goal here is not to make value judgments but to foster self-reflection and self-awareness in order to develop mutually beneficial capabilities for self-monitoring and self-evaluating teaching acts. As Jo Ann Crandall (2000: 35) observes, peer observation, done properly and purposefully by two collaborating teachers, should

> be thought of as a cooperative discovery process. A focus on shared students and their attempts to negotiate meaning and construct understandings in both classes can help keep the attention focused on student learning, rather than on teacher effectiveness.

Working together, colleagues can create a conducive atmosphere where teamwork is encouraged, and where they help each other improve both the work environment and their own teaching effectiveness.

6.4 A Case of and for *Seeing-that*

The above discussion on the concept of seeing, and on the multiple perspectives of learners, teachers, and observers leads us to believe that systematic observation of teaching and learning will provide a well-rounded, stereoscopic picture of the intended and unintended goals and outcomes of classroom events and activities. But, what we should be focusing on is not any form of observation but specifically the *seeing-that* form of observation. Recall from the early part of this chapter that *seeing-that* is a higher form of observation involving a dynamic relationship between seeing and knowing. *Seeing-that* form of classroom observation presents all the participating individuals with a view of classroom learning and teaching that they may not have been paying attention to before. It helps them focus on a variety of experiences, attitudes, beliefs, values, and identities that they all bring to the classroom.

Such a *seeing-that* form of observation can be realized through a three-tier process I have discussed elsewhere (Kumaravadivelu 1999b, 2003b): (a) pre-observation; (b) observation of lessons; and (c) post-observation. During the pre-observation stage, the observer elicits from the teacher information about the specific objectives of the class to be observed, and how the teacher proposes to achieve those objectives. The observer reviews the information and also takes a look at the textbook and other materials to be used in class. During the next stage, the observer observes the designated lesson and videotapes the class, and takes notes on specific interactional episodes to be jointly explored later with the teacher. During the post-observation stage, the teacher brings to the conversation table notes on interactional episodes to be explored further with the observer. The observer and the teacher discuss the selected interactional episodes and exchange their perspectives. They then meet with a group of learners who figured in the episodes selected for analysis, and try to seek learner perspectives on those episodes. They pull together all three perspectives (teacher, learner, observer) to make sense of what they have observed.

The above observational procedure usually raises two related concerns. One is videotaping. There may indeed be some logistical concerns but the benefits easily outweigh them. Availability of a video camera is not generally a problem because most educational institutions have them. The observer can easily set it up and operate it, or, if that is a hassle, a tripod can be used and placed in a strategic position in the classroom. Any learner distraction from the presence of a camera (or of the observer) wears off after a few minutes of the start of the class. The well-known benefits of videotaping a lesson include: the participants can watch the videotape at a convenient time; they can focus on specific students, on specific episodes, and watch them again and again; and they can easily get a critical view of the nature of input and interaction in the class. The second issue is time. It is generally conceded that just setting up and using the video camera is not really time consuming, but transcription is. A viable solution is not to transcribe the entire lesson but only episodes selected for analysis and interpretation, which are normally short. In fact, transcription of even short, selected episodes becomes necessary only if the participants intend to publish a paper or write a report based on their observation. An important pedagogic advantage is for the teacher to play selected episodes back to the whole class and initiate a meaningful conversation with learners, seeking their interpretation and feedback.

By way of illustrating the contours of a *seeing-that* form of observation and the multiplicity of perspectives, I present below two examples: one relates to teacher-learner interaction in an ESL classroom, and the other to student teacher-teacher educator dialogue in the context of the practicum.

Consider the following interaction that occurred in an ESL reading comprehension class (reported in Kumaravadivelu 2003b). The teacher was planning to use a lesson titled "Looking for an apartment." As part of the classroom conversation, she started asking her learners what factors they would consider before choosing an apartment in which to live; factors such as proximity to campus, safe neighborhood, monthly rent, size of the house, or whether there are good schools nearby to send their children to, etc. Here is a short episode dealing with the last factor (the numbers indicate turn numbers in the communication sequence; T = Teacher S = Student):

51. T: OK, so ... S 13, what is most important to you? Size of the house? The quality of the school system?
52. S13:   The quality of the school system.
53. S14:   School system?
54. T: Yah, why did you choose that?
55. S13:   My children at home ...
56. S14:   I don't understand school system.
57. T: OK, he has children that live with him at home. So ... that's the most important to him. OK ... ?
58. S14:   I am confused.
59. T: All right, all right. You're confused. Let's get unconfused. His children go to school, so he wants to live near a school ... OK? ... Now, you tell me ... what's the most important to you?
60. S14:   (Still looking puzzled) ... Um ... close to work.

61. S15:   (Turning to S14) You got no work (students laugh).
62. T: That's funny. … (the conversation continues).

As is evident, in turn 52, S13 expresses the opinion that the quality of the school system would be his first consideration for deciding on an apartment. S14 asks, without any emphasis on any of the words, "Why school system?" The teacher thought that S14 was actually addressing S13, asking him in effect why the school system was his first consideration. That's why she reinforced the question to S13: "Yah, why did you choose that?" And S13 replies suitably. He has school-going children (turn 55). Now, S14 says: "I don't understand." The teacher tries to explain: "He has children that live with him at home. So, that's the most important to him." But, S14 is not giving up. "I am confused," he says. The teacher, clearly irritated, says sternly "All right, all right. You're confused. Let's get unconfused. His children go to school, so he wants to live near a school … OK?" By that time, S14 lost all interest and that's why, when the teacher asked him for his most important consideration for renting an apartment, he nonchalantly responds "close to work" even though he doesn't have any part-time work, something that his friend S15 (turn 61) gleefully points out.

When in class, the observer did not have a clue of what was happening. But she teased it out after talking to the teacher and S14, who incidentally is one of the bright students in the class. Here's the deconstructed version: In turn 53, S14 asks: "Why school system?" That was not a question addressed to S13, as was thought by the teacher. That was a question addressed to the teacher herself. S14 wanted to know why the word "system" is used in relation to "school." He wanted to know why it is called a "school *system*." The emphasis is on system even though he did not emphasize it. Now, the teacher, knowing fully well that S14 is a bright student, thought that he was just being mischievous as usual. She didn't think that he was really confused. That's why she got irritated and said, "get unconfused." Later, when the student told her that he didn't really understand the phrase *school system,* she was very apologetic. She explained that the word *system* is used to refer to a cluster of schools managed and run by a central authority within a county, all having a common curriculum.

The reconstruction of even a short episode like this demonstrates how a micro-analysis of interaction between teachers and learners done with sensitivity to learner, teacher, and observer perspectives can help the participants look beyond the surface and see what is actually going on. It is rather evident from the above that teachers must learn to see what goes in their classroom, and see it in a systematic and sus-tained manner. Only then will they be able to theorize from their classroom. They must first develop the knowledge and skill necessary to engage in the *seeing-that* form of critical classroom observation. The time to start is when they are enrolled in their teacher education program. Any viable teacher education program, then, must introduce to student teachers classroom observation frameworks that offer new possibilities of and procedures for critically self-observing, self-analyzing, and self-evaluating teaching acts.

The following example illustrates what shape the *seeing-that* form of observation can probably take in the case of a TESOL practicum class involving pre–observation and post–observation dialogues between teacher educators and student teachers. As I discuss this case, readers will be able to see how closely related the *seeing-that* form of observation is to the process of dialogizing (specifically to dialogic inquiry in the Bakhtinian sense) discussed in Chapter 5. At the time of video data collection, the teacher educator, a 51-year old female professor in a state university in California, was teaching Methodology, and the Practicum, both part of a graduate program in TESOL. The student teacher involved was a 25-year old male graduate student. The class he was teaching for his teaching practice consisted largely of Vietnamese refugee students of mixed English proficiency level who were learning both ESL and job skills simultaneously.

During the pre–observation stage, the teacher educator (TE) meets with the student teacher (ST). At this meeting, the ST informs the TE about learning objectives, teaching strategies, instructional materials, etc. Then, the lesson is videotaped while the TE observes the class. Throughout the lesson, the TE notes down critical points of where the lesson is going well and where it is lacking. A post-observation is held two days after the lesson. In the meantime, the ST has viewed the videotape of the lesson and is prepared to comment on and ask questions about certain segments that he felt were notable in some way. The TE likewise selects from her list of critical moments those that she deems most important to talk about. What I would like to highlight here is how pre- and post-observation sessions establish a meaningful focus for the whole dialogic experience, one that is jointly constructed by the ST and the TE. What is crucial here are not the activities themselves, but the dialogic nature of these activities that are characteristic of a *seeing-that* form of observation.

Owing to an earlier talk, the TE knows that the ST plans to introduce and help learners practice conversational exchanges given in the prescribed textbook. She notices a mismatch between the language used in "real life" situations and the fabricated authenticity found in the textbook. Believing as she does in the dialogic approach, she decides to draw the student-teacher into a dialogic discourse rather than tell him what she thinks should be done. The following segment from the pre-observation conversation shows how the two interlocutors entered into a dialogic mode in order to address the issue (TE = Teacher Educator, ST = Student Teacher, and three dots (...) means a short pause):

01 TE: Yeah, let me just ask you your opinion on, on one thing ... one thing that I, uh, have struggled with is, uh, balancing the grammatical competence with the communicative competence and, uh, in terms of uhm, having students, say "Oh, did you clean this? Yes, I cleaned it," I think, you know the reality is that if you were to ask that question probably the answer would be something like "Yeah sure," you know, without that past tense form. So I-, I'm just wondering what your, your take on that is.

02 ST: Uhm, well, I think, uhm, (clears throat) you mean uh, in terms of like what real communication is?

03 TE: Yeah

04 ST: In terms of what's, what's being, being presented in the actual material that we're using?

05 TE: Yeah

06 ST: I think that, that, me personally, I don't really differen-, differentiate between that now at this point in my career, but think I would be, would eventually. At this point I think I'm kind of like using the text material, to help me, uh, get through a lesson.

07 TE: Uh huh

08 ST: You know … (clears throat)

09 TE: Yeah

10 ST: But every now and then, I stop, and, I don't know, every now and then, that's not a very good definition of when exactly …

11 TE: Yeah, yeah

12 ST: But it does come about when I, when I actually say to students, "We really don't say this, in English,"

13 TE: Uh huh, uh huh

14 ST: What you'll hear is, and this, this happens actually, you know, almost every week, like a student will say, uhm, we'll have a long full-sentence question …

15 TE: Uh huh

16 ST: … and I'll, and I'll, I'll expect a full-sentence answer, but the students will, will, for example, yesterday in class, "What is the, the ingredient that's listed the most in this soup?" and … I wanted to get, you know, a, a complete answer, and one student said, "beef stock!" and I said, "Well, that's fine" That's exactly what, you know, an acceptable answer is in English, but for, for a complete sentence, it's a lot longer, and it wastes a lot, a lot of time … that's what you're getting at?

17 TE: Yeah, that's it exactly.

18 ST: What's my stance on that?

19 TE: Yeah

20 ST: (clears throat) I think it's important to know that, but I think it's also important to use those examples in the book just to familiarize themselves with that type of language.

21 TE: Uh huh

22 ST: Because even if they don't use that in, the, you know, communication, you know, on a day to day basis …

23 TE: Uh huh

24 ST: At least they're familiar with what those, words sound like.

25 TE: Uh huh

26 ST: You know, they may not be that important in, in uh, communication, but at, at this point in, in their their language learning ability, but eventually it may be.

27 TE: Uh huh, yeah.

(Data source: Author)

This pre-observation segment reveals a number of stances in the dialogic discourse between the TE and the ST. First, by sharing with her ST her own struggle to balance grammatical usage with communicative use, the TE has created a climate in which both participants can function as co-equals. How to bridge the gap between prefabricated textbook language and "natural" language is a challenge which virtually all L2 teachers face. After having aligned herself with the ST in foregrounding this situation, the TE solicits the ST's input.

Second, in asking the ST to reflect on his position on this particular issue, the TE's motive is to discover what the ST's real instructional objective is—is it communicative authenticity, grammatical nicety, vocabulary expansion, or is it something else? What the ST seems to be saying here is that he is prepared to sacrifice a certain degree of naturalness in speech in order to foreground the structure and vocabulary of English in settings that might be relevant for this job-oriented English class (turn 20), even though the main focus of the class is communication.

Third, it becomes clear that, although the question of "authenticity" has been frequently discussed in the Methodology as well as in the Practicum classes, the ST hasn't really thought this issue through, not even when preparing his lesson plan. What the TE is doing in this dialogic exchange is encouraging the ST's introspective thoughts in an atmosphere of minimal dialogic tension. This eventually (after a lengthy conversation involving 17 turns) leads the ST to the realization that the TE has indeed asked for his personal opinion on the issue. In turn 18, he asks with a rising intonation: "What's my stance on that?" and then proceeds to articulate his thoughts.

Finally, this episode also reveals the TE's willingness to help the ST create and defend his identity, his voice. This is crucial because by supporting his voice, she discovers not only his pedagogical orientation but also the practical motivation underlying it. In accordance with Bakhtinian dialogic inquiry, the TE has thus created a safe and nurturing environment which accommodates more than one view, more than one meaning, more than one belief system.

During the post-observation dialogue, the question of authentic communication is taken up once again in part because during the lesson, in addition to repeating the conversational routines given in the textbook, some students use "natural" sentence fragments. Consider this segment in which the ST himself raises the issue:

01 ST: Yeah, if I might just ask, actually, just comment on, on what we had talked about before, uh, one of the last questions, you asked me how this kind of conversation fits into real life communication …

02 TE: Uh huh

03 ST: You know, I'm aware that, that, that distinction is there … a lot of what's taught? You know, what's really needed? Etcetera …

04 TE: Yeah

05 ST: There's a big difference there … but I don't really focus on that a lot, you know, but I do know it, it exists, that distinction … but I think that a lot of the

times, uhm, my own personal teaching style, shows them that there is the difference there ... I don't, you know, explicitly come out and state it, that there is a difference ... I don't know if that's confusing for a lot of students? You know, uh, this was something that I was having a hard time with ... but, I think, some of the learners, ... some of them are high-beginning to low-intermediate, I think they know what's ... what's going on and I think the other students are at a stage right now in their language learning where they don't really understand a whole lot anyway ... you know, and, I try to slow down a little bit to catch them ... you know, this is the whole, speeding-up and slowing-down pacing thing again but ...

06 TE: Yeah

07 ST: I'm pretty comfortable with it ... you know, I don't know if it's comfortable for them, but I think that's one of the bigger questions, so ...

08 TE: Yeah, actually, I thought you handled it very well because you used intonation, to make it work ... uh, for example, the question was uh, "Did I wash the dishes very well?" and you said, "Yes, you did. You washed them very well." and your intonation was very, natural, and it works with the, structure so I think that, you know, you wanna, minimize the, the difference between ... you know ... what's really out there and still give them an opportunity to work on something ... and I thought that was a good solution to this.

09 ST: And that's not intentional ... and that just happens.

10 TE: Yeah.

11 ST: So I don't know if that, where that came from ... but maybe I've seen somebody do that before ...

12 TE: Yeah

13 ST: ... and I, and I thought, thought it worked pretty well, or something ... I don't know.

14 TE: Uh huh ... but, see ... now you can ... make that a ... a conscious strategy from now on ...

15 ST: Uh huh

16 TE: ... to use the intonation ... uh, let's see, for example, if someone said uh, you know, "Did, did you enjoy that movie, Peter?" and you could say, "Yeah, I did I, I really enjoyed it a lot" ... and then you're getting the past tense in there, but it sounds totally natural.

17 ST: Uh huh

18 TE: So I think it's only when ... sometimes, you'll see books where, the answer is, "Did you enjoy the movie?" "Yes, I did. I really enjoyed the movie,"

19 ST: Uh huh

20 TE: And it's pretty mechanical ... but you can transform that into something more natural.

21 ST: One of the things I do do, uhm, when we get into these, fabricated, unau-, uh, not authentic conversations?

22 TE: Uh huh

23 ST: And I find students reading them like this, this is "How are you doing today?" "I'm doing fine. How are you?" "I'm fine, thank you—it's nice to see you again, great!"

24 TE: Uh huh

25 ST: I explain to them that's Robo-Student, and I read it back to them as Teacher, and they all laugh and chuckle and then they, you know, I'll get a couple of the other students who I can … I know who are using more intonation … and they'll give an example … and I'll really overemphasize it, "How are you doing today?" you know, and I'll, I'll really get into the intona-tion but when I catch them being monotone (snaps fingers) immediately it kinda triggers something in me that that's not the way we speak so, I mean, intona-tion's always been kind of big for me. I even sense, you know, just the beginning here so, I don't know why that is but it just seems to work and you said making a conscious, kind a teaching strategy out of it. I think it'll work … really well for me.

(Data source: Author)

What is unfolding in this dialogic interaction is a respectful and meaningful exchange of ideas between the TE and the ST, resulting in the latter's increased awareness of what actually occurs in the classroom. This increased awareness ulti-mately leads to a shift in his pedagogic stance. Initially, he does not seem to be conscious of a particular technique that he has been using to reduce the perceived gap between the artificial language in the textbook and "real-life" language. In turn 5, he says that he doesn't "really focus on that a lot." When the TE points out (turn 8) that he is actually using intonation as strategy to reduce the gap, he asserts that the strategy was "not intentional" (turn 9). Undeterred by his assertion, the TE gives him another example and suggests that he use intonation as a conscious strategy (turns 14–20). Then, suddenly, in what appears to be a moment of self-revelation, the ST is able to recognize the discrepancy between what he thinks has been hap-pening and what has actually been happening in his classes. He is now able to recognize and acknowledge what he has been doing all along: "intonation's always been kind of big for me" (turn 25). That revelation gives him his identity, his voice, his confidence: "I think it'll work … really well for me" (turn 25).

This episode clearly shows that when a *seeing-that* form of observational dialogue is created for STs, and when they are granted a reasonable amount of control over what and how they will teach, they get an opportunity to find their own identity and express their own voice. This form of observation also provides opportunities for TEs to better understand the discourse of their STs, which in turn could lead to a better understanding of the possibilities and limitations of their own pedagogic values. This kind of seeing demonstrates the potential to prompt a reexamination of one's pedagogic beliefs thereby discovering something different about one's Self. It also develops a deeper understanding of the relationship between seeing and knowing. It is certainly true that this form of observation does not eliminate the power inequality inherent in the relationship between STs and TEs. But, it does allow the interlocutors to reach what Bakhtin calls "responsive understanding."

6.5 In Closing

I started this chapter with a brief philosophical rendering of the concept of seeing, borrowed from Kvernbekk. We learned that we are all habituated to look rather than to see, and that there can be at least three different forms of seeing: *seeing-in, seeing-as*, and *seeing-that*. We also learned that *seeing-that* is a higher form of seeing, one that is critically mediated by seeing and knowing, something that helps us forge new connections between our conceptual knowledge and perceptual knowledge. I then referred to three classroom observational approaches—interaction approach, discourse approach, and critical approach, expanding the third in terms of critical classroom discourse analysis. Connecting the three observational approaches to the three forms of seeing, I surmised a tentative link between interaction approach and *seeing-in*, between discourse approach and *seeing-as*, and between critical approach and *seeing-that*. A true understanding of the classroom entails engaging in the *seeing-that* form of observation.

Moving along, I emphasized the need to consider at least three different but inter-related perspectives to any classroom actor or activity: learner perspective that recognizes learners as important stakeholders in the business of learning and teaching, teacher perspective that recognizes the power and authority vested in the teacher and the asymmetrical relationship between teachers and learners, and observer perspective that recognizes the crucial role observers could play in offering valuable insights about language lessons. I then provided methodological procedures and illustrative examples for doing the *seeing-that* form of observation—one in the context of learner-teacher interaction, and another in the context of teacher educator-student teacher dialogue. The examples show how the *seeing-that* form of observation is capable of assisting participants to make the connection between seeing and knowing. I emphasized that given the importance of seeing what happens in the classroom, teacher education programs have a responsibility to introduce to student teachers classroom observation frameworks that offer new possibilities of and procedures for seeing the classroom with clarity and creativity.

Rapid Reader Response

Write a quick response to the following questions. Form small groups, share your thoughts, and discuss them with other members of the group.

1 What is the one big point you learned from this chapter?
2 What is the one main unanswered question you leave the chapter with?
3 What is the one surprising idea or concept you encountered in this chapter?
4 What is the one example of terminology or concept you do not fully understand?

Reflective tasks

Task 6.1 Learner Metaphors

T6.1.1 Rod Ellis (2001) has compiled from the SLA literature several metaphors to characterize learner roles. I have included seven of them in this chapter: learner as container, machine, negotiator, problem-solver, builder, investor, and struggler. Go back to the text and read the brief descriptions associated with each of these metaphors.

T6.1.2 Recall your days as a learner. Which of the metaphors (there can be more than one) best describe you as a learner? Think about a few specific instances of your learner behavior that will fit in with the metaphor(s) you self-selected.

T6.1.3 To what extent do you think the metaphors associated with yourself shaped your and your teachers' expectations of your classroom behavior?

T6.1.4 In your view, is it advantageous or disadvantageous to engage in metaphorical representations of learners? In what way?

Task 6.2 Teacher Metaphors

T6.2.1 Farrell (2011) has identified three major clusters of identities for teachers: teacher as manager, acculturator, and professional, with a number of sub-identities under each. Go back to the text and read the brief descriptions associated with each of these metaphors.

T6.2.2 If you are a practicing teacher, would you describe yourself as a manager, an acculturator, or a professional (you can be more than one)? If you are a student teacher, think about a few of your teachers and say how you would describe them.

T6.2.3 To what extent do you think the metaphors associated with yourself (or your teachers) shaped your (or your teachers') teaching behavior?

T6.2.4 In your view, is it advantageous or disadvantageous to engage in metaphorical representations of teachers? In what way?

Task 6.3 Seeing, What?

T6.3.1 In this chapter, we came across *seeing-in*, *seeing-as*, and *seeing-that* forms of observation. What do these forms mean to you personally?

T6.3.2 Based on whatever classroom observation you may have done, how would you describe the form of observation you followed, or asked to follow?

T6.3.3 What form of observation did (does) the teacher education program you were (are) associated with focus on, and how do you know that?

T6.3.4 Do you agree that the *seeing-that* form of observation is the best form of observation? Why?

Task 6.4 Seeing, What For?

T6.4.1 One of the student teachers referred to in the chapter (by Orland-Barak and Leshem 2009) is reported to have said: "We have already spent 12 years in school and now when we go to school again we feel that everything is familiar and nothing is really being added ... " Reflect on this remark.

T6.4.2 Did you have a similar or a different experience when you were asked to observe lessons as a student teacher? Explain.

T6.4.3 When you were asked to observe lessons taught by your teacher educator, master teacher, or a co-operating teacher, what exactly was already "familiar" to you?

T6.4.4 When you were asked to observe lessons taught by your teacher educator, master teacher or a co-operating teacher, did you add anything new to your initial knowledge-base? If so, what?

Exploratory Project

Project 6.1 Learning by Seeing

This project is designed to help you articulate what you think you learn when you observe a lesson taught by yourself, your teacher educator, master teacher, cooperating teacher, or a colleague.

P6.1.1 If you are a practicing teacher, arrange to videotape one of your lessons, and ask one of your colleagues to be an observer. If you are student teacher, observe and videotape (with permission) a lesson taught by your teacher educator, master teacher, cooperating teacher, or a classmate. Try to follow the three-tier observational procedure (pre-observation, observation, and post-observation) outlined in the chapter.

P6.1.2 Focus on (a) input (i.e., teacher talk and learner talk); (b) interaction (i.e., turn taking/turn giving techniques, and the content and style of interaction); and (c) strategies teachers and learners use to maximize learning potential in the class. Select a few episodes that appear to showcase learning opportunities created (or missed) by the teacher.

P6.1.3 Show the selected episodes to learners who figured in them, and to the observer. Ask them what they think actually happened in these episodes.

P6.1.4 Identify the similarities and dissimilarities in the three (learner, teacher, and observer) perspectives.

P6.1.5 How do you account for the dissimilarities you find in the three perspectives?

P6.1.6 How would you describe your observational analysis: *seeing-in, seeing-as, seeing-that,* or a combination of all three?

P6.1.7 Write a brief report of your observation. If you wish, use the following to trigger your writing process (Orland-Barak & Leshem 2009: 24):

I was surprised to discover ... and I have learned that ...
I have changed my mind about ... because ...
I was reinforced to find that ... therefore ...
I was reminded of ... and that has made me think ...

P6.1.8 Reflect on, and briefly write about, what you learned by doing this project.

7

(RE)MAKING A MODULAR MODEL

The human mind moves always forward, alters its viewpoint and enlarges its thought substance, and the effect of these changes is to render past systems of thinking obsolete or, when they are preserved, to extend, to modify and subtly or visibly to alter their value.

(Sri Aurobindo, 1939/2001: 131)

7.0 Introduction

In this globalized and globalizing world, it's time for language teachers and teacher educators to move forward, alter viewpoints, enlarge thought substance, and render some of the past systems obsolete. It may appear to be an indomitable task, but it is not an intractable one. What then do language teachers and teacher educators have to do to accomplish the task? The essentials of a modular model presented in the preceding pages is an attempt to respond to that question by saying: teachers have to understand (a) how to build a viable professional, personal, and procedural knowledge base; (b) how to explore learners' needs, motivation, and autonomy; (c) how to recognize their own identities, beliefs, and values; (d) how to do the right kind of teaching, theorizing, and dialogizing; and (e) how to see their own teaching acts by taking into account learner, teacher, and observer perspectives on classroom events and activities. By extension, teacher educators also have the responsibility to create the conditions necessary for teachers to know, to analyze, to recognize, to do, and to see what constitutes learning, teaching, and teacher development.

Grounded on the operating principles of particularity, practicality, and possibility, and erected on the pillars of postnational, postmodern, postcolonial, post-transmission, and postmethod perspectives that have emerged from global studies in the humanities and social sciences, the modular model presents a cohesive and comprehensive framework for language teacher education for a global society. In this concluding chapter, I reflect on the prospects and problems of designing a context-sensitive model for language teacher education. I will start with a brief note on the nature of models and modules to clear any potential misunderstanding about the use of these terms. I will then consider possible ways of designing and delivering a model that is sensitive to local exigencies and global demands. I will also touch upon the challenge of change facing any innovative educational endeavor before closing the chapter (indeed, the book) with a few contemplative thoughts.

7.1 Models and Modules

I have ventured to call my framework for language teacher education a *modular model*, thereby coupling two terms that invoke varied interpretations in various disciplines. Model building is a very common practice in natural, physical, and social sciences. Aspiring or claiming to be predictive, most models in these fields make use of mathematical, statistical, or computational logarithms. Because of the multiplicity of models, and methods of model making, there is very little consensus about what models are, how they should be designed, or what we are supposed to learn from them. I find a simple depiction of models presented in the popular textbook *An Introduction to Models in the Social Sciences* written by Charles Lave and James March very useful for my purpose. "A model," according to them,

> is a simplified picture of a part of the real world. It has some of the characteristics of a real world, but not all of them. It is a set of interrelated guesses about the world. Like all pictures, a model is simpler than the phenomena it is supposed to represent or explain.
>
> *(1993: 3)*

It is difficult, indeed impossible, to capture the full complexity of the world, and hence a model will forever remain a simplified representation of the world. This is particularly true of the world of education with so many contexts, players, and variables most of which cannot be neatly controlled for any investigative endeavor that could even remotely be labeled scientific.

I make no pretensions about scientific rigor regarding the essentials of a modular model I have presented; but, the entire enterprise is marked by a scientific temper that demands robust inferential reasoning. The result is a conceptual model of an explanatory kind that aims at interpreting the world of language teacher education in all its complexity and multidimensionality. Interpretation is the key for this kind of conceptual model making. Interpretation need not be scientific so long as it is intellectually rigorous. That is what we learn from cultural anthropologist Clifford Geertz, who chides his fellow anthropologists for pretending to be hardcore scientists. "Social scientists," he says, did not need to be mimic physicists or closet humanists or to invent some new realm of being to serve as the object of their investigations. Instead they could proceed with their vocation, trying to discover order in collective life, and decide how what they were doing was connected to related enterprises when they managed to get some of it done; and many of them have taken an essentially hermeneutic, if that word frightens, conjuring up images of biblical zealots, literary humbugs, and Teutonic professors, an "interpretive" approach to their task.

(1983: 21)

Discovering order in collective life, or finding *the pattern that connects*, to use a familiar phrase from yet another anthropologist, Gregory Bateson, is what I have tried to do. I have collected and synthesized discrete and disparate insights from the professional literature primarily in the fields of education and TESOL. I have clustered the insights into five constituent parts—knowing, analyzing, recognizing, doing, and seeing. I have called these constituent parts, modules.

The term *modules,* like *models,* is used variously in many disciplines. In *The Logics of Social Structure,* sociologist Kytiakos Kontopoulos defines modules and modularity. For him, modularity means that

a would-be system can (a) achieve a degree of closure and can be seen as behaving independently or, at least, semi-independently of the surrounding conditions (semi-closed); and that (b) this system is seen as becoming a modular component of a larger semi-closed system, which itself may have achieved a degree of closure, and so on.

(1993: 32)

In other words, a module is an independent as well as an interdependent component (or a sub-system), several of which can be integrated into an overarching model which, in turn, functions as an independent and interdependent larger system. Both the sub-systems and the larger system are self-sustaining at one level and are reliant on others at another.

To relate the notion of modularity to the model presented in this book, notice that each of the five modules—knowing, analyzing, recognizing, doing, and seeing—constitutes a sub-system that is grouped along with others to form a larger system, a model for language teacher education. Each of the five modules is seen as independent as well as interdependent. It is independent in the sense that each can stand on its own in terms of its specific goals and expected outcomes. It is interdependent in the sense that each shapes and is shaped by the other. Each has an identifiable function, and at the same time each draws its sustenance from its dependence on others. Thus, the model constitutes a network of mutually reinforcing as well as mutually restraining sub-systems.

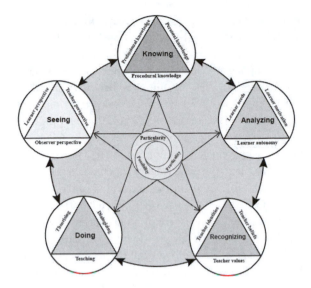

From a conceptual point of view, then, the model presents a dynamic network of modules that interact in a complex way. The centrality of the model lies in the process of forging a synergic relationship where the whole is much more than the sum of the parts. That is, working together, they generate a richness of experiences and outcomes that are considerably greater than the experiences and outcomes not obtainable by any one of them working alone. From a practical point of view, the dynamism of the model renders it flexible enough to help present and prospective teachers to meet the challenges of learning and teaching needs and wants and situations that are unpredictably numerous. Thus, the essentials of the model presented here show a pathway towards the design and delivery of a context-sensitive model that local practitioners should be able to build.

7.2 Design and Delivery

An important caveat that should always be kept in mind is that the modular model as presented here offers no more than a skeletal framework for the development of a context-sensitive language teacher education program. It is up to local practitioners, taking into account the particularity of the local historical, political, social, educational, and institutional exigencies, to add the right type of flesh and blood to the skeletal framework so as to activate it in a way that best serves local needs, wants, and situations. In the course of designing and delivering, local practitioners can use the essentials of the model as broad guidelines to conceive and construct what they consider to be a locally relevant language teacher education program. They can also use it as a compass to check the direction to know where they have been, where they are, and which way they should be heading.

In order not to lose direction during the process of designing a context-sensitive program, it is worthwhile to keep in mind certain fundamental tenets of the modular model. First and foremost, the model recognizes that neither knowledge nor knowledge development exists in neat, discrete categories but rather in amorphous, intertwined modules. What this means is that, if we take the essentials of the model seriously, we need to move away from the traditional way of designing discrete, content-based courses, and move towards designing holistic, process-based modules. Currently, as was mentioned in Chapter 1, many language teacher education programs, with very few exceptions, offer a series of discrete courses in language structures, learning theories, teaching methods, curriculum development, testing techniques, etc. In the name of moving away from such a traditional approach, we should not deceive ourselves by merely clustering, as some teacher education programs have done, a couple of courses related to introductory linguistics and call the cluster "Language Module," or cluster a couple of courses related to second language acquisition and call the cluster "Learning Module," etc. A true modular model demands that we cross these artificial boundaries that have been put in place more for logistical than for logical reasons, and, instead, conceive a module in terms of knowing, analyzing, recognizing, doing, or seeing. For instance, a Knowing Module should focus on the processes of acquiring professional, personal, and procedural knowledge about language structures, language acquisition, language teaching methods, classroom communication, etc. in an integrated manner.

Yet another tenet of the modular model demands that we move away from the traditional single, linear path regarding entry points and exit points in a teacher education program. Currently, in most teacher education programs, student teachers often start with a couple of introductory courses in language and linguistics, sequentially move along the assembly line of other discrete courses, and usually end up with a capstone course in practicum. In other words, there is one entry point and there is one exit point. The modular model envisages multiple entry points and multiple exit points, that is to say, a particular teacher education program can begin and end with a particular module depending on the needs, wants, and abilities of a given group of student teachers or practicing teachers.

In addition to these two basic tenets, the essentials of the modular model have been discussed and illustrated throughout the preceding chapters. The question, however, remains: what exactly are the specific strategies or steps that might profitably be followed if one wishes to design and deliver a context-sensitive modular model for language teacher education? There are several sources one can turn to for inspiration. One interesting source that I find useful and useable, and one that I strongly recommend to interested readers, is Ideo (pronounced *eye-dee-oh*). It is an award-winning global design firm that takes "a human-centered approach" to help organizations and individuals in the public and private sectors to innovate and grow. The firm has pioneered what is called *design thinking*, a new perspective to the process and practice of designing. Design thinking is a mindset. Thinking like a designer can transform the way you approach the world when imagining and creating new solutions for the future: it's about being aware of the world around you, believing that you play a role in shaping that world, and taking action toward a more desirable future.

Design thinking can be employed in many areas of human endeavor (e.g., art and science) and at many levels (e.g., macro and micro).

In order to specifically help educators, the firm has just released a freely downloadable digital toolkit called *Design Thinking for Educators* (Ideo 2011, Version One, April 2011. All the citations dealing with design thinking, including the one given above, are taken from this new release; for a full report go to www.ideo.com and follow the link). In it, the firm recognizes that "the challenges educators are confronted with are real, complex and varied. As such, they require new perspectives, new tools, and new approaches." Accordingly, it offers practical tips for educators to hone their skills in design process.

Basically, the design process is structured in five phases starting from identifying a challenge to finding and building a solution. They are:

- discovery (building a solid foundation for ideas, and opening up to new opportunities);
- interpretation (finding meaning in what is observed, and turning it into actionable opportunities);
- ideation (brainstorming for ideas, and sparking useable thoughts);
- experimentation (making ideas tangible, and building rough prototypes); and
- evolution (planning next steps, and documenting the process).

Each phase is divided into skills which are further subdivided into sub-skills. According to the toolkit, the design process is best achieved through teamwork, requiring the team to pause at every step to reflect, analyze, evaluate, think again, and then evolve.

I borrow some of the broad ideas from the toolkit and try to relate them specifically to designing a context-sensitive modular model for language teacher education. What follows is not a comprehensive design procedure; therefore, it would be beneficial to go to Ideo's website for more details. In order to ensure a focused explanation, I address the following steps mainly to interested language teacher educators. The steps are couched in imperative terms only to connote their operational character and not to convey any prescriptive quality.

At the first phase of discovery, the goal is to build a solid foundation for ideas and expectations. Form an informal team of interested teacher educators drawing from within one's own institution, and, if possible, across close-by institutions, making sure a culture of collaboration will prevail. As a team, define and understand the challenge by sharing knowledge and experience about the strengths and weaknesses of the current teacher education program in place, and the possible windows of opportunity opened up by the essentials of the modular model presented in this book. A concrete outcome at this phase could just be a bank of questions that problematize what is being done and what should be done.

The goal of the second phase—interpretation—is to find meaning in what has been shared and observed, and come out with an outline of actionable thoughts. Focus on the five modules—knowing, analyzing, recognizing, doing, and seeing—one by one, and try to find themes and topics for each of the modules in order to make sense of research findings (some of which are reviewed in the relevant chapters). For instance, with regard to the Knowing Module, one possible talking/decision point is: to what extent can the importance attached to the development of student teachers' personal knowledge base be translated into a workable proposition given the resources and constraints associated with the institutions and student teacher populations that the team members serve? A concrete outcome at this phase could be to arrive at a frame of opportunities that includes ideas for further action.

At the next phase of ideation, take some of the proposed actionable thoughts on any aspect of a module, and brainstorm further in order to narrow down thoughts that are promising. Build on them to refine them. Do a quick reality check in terms of what part of the promising thoughts could be transformed into actionable plans. For instance, going back to the personal knowledge segment of the Knowing Module, we learned that teachers' personal knowledge involves the ability to critically recognize, reflect, review and reinvent their own identities, beliefs, and values (as we saw in Chapters 1 and 4). If that is the case, what kind of an actionable plan will help student teachers develop such abilities? A concrete outcome at this stage could be a tentative blueprint of tasks, activities, and projects that could activate the problem-solving and practical reasoning capabilities of student teachers.

The fourth phase—experimentation—should not be mistaken to mean highly sophisticated, variable-controlled, scientific research. For our purpose, it merely involves putting together some of the actionable plans, and building rough prototypes of tasks, activities, and projects that can be pilot tested. Its main purpose is to get meaningful and useable feedback. To quote from the Ideo website, the experimentation part "creates a real space to try something new. It gives you permission to fail and to learn from your mistakes, because you come up with new ideas, get feedback on them, *then* iterate." The team, then, has to identify reliable sources for feedback, administer the tasks and activities, and collect useable feedback. In order to do that in an effective way, it may be necessary to build focused and pointed questions that facilitate thoughtful answers from respondents. A concrete outcome at this phase could be a set of specific learning opportunities that the experimentation might provide for the team.

The fifth and final phase—evolution—is aimed at documenting the process and the progress, and using them for further decision-making. Specifically, this phase involves integrating the collected feedback, defining success or failure, and building on the experience. It may lead to a review and reformulation of some parts of the design process and procedure in order to satisfy the expectations of the team as well as other stakeholders. Finally, it involves identifying what needs to be done next in terms of dissemination and implementation of the tested and verified ideas and insights.

The five phases of design process described in relation to language teacher education require sustained conversation and constructive criticism carried out in a collaborative spirit in a collegial atmosphere (cf: *learning conversations* in Chapter 5). Design thinking, warn the originators of the Ideo toolkit for educators,

> may seem very straightforward at first glance, but there is one important aspect to understand: its real value lies in the mix of tangible problem solving and abstract thinking. The very concrete observations of the first phase are abstracted as you define themes and insights. Only after you have developed a sense of meaning and direction do you develop tangible solutions.

In order to develop tangible solutions, and put them together in a meaningful way to design a context-sensitive modular model, language teacher educators need to pay special attention to the governing principles of particularity, practicality, and possibility (cf: Chapter 1). Local contextual factors will determine the goal and the content of language teacher education which, in turn, will shape the contours of a model. Consequently, there cannot be any one overarching modular model that results from a top-down exercise, ready to be imposed by a center authority, and ready to be implemented by a periphery. Any such centralized attempt is bound to be futile. As stated earlier, this and other preceding chapters attempt to provide only general guidelines, a broad roadmap that can lead to the designing of a context-sensitive model. Ultimately, it is up to local practitioners to take up the challenge, build a suitable model, and change the current ways of doing language teacher education.

7.3 Challenge and Change

Given the enormity and complexity of the task, it is easy and normal to develop resistance to change. The challenge of change may be particularly acute in an educational environment where teachers and teacher educators hardly have any incentive or motivation to embark on a critical and continual examination of issues big and small. In such an environment, there is very little space for bottom-up deliberation and decision-making. Besides, in many cases, change can produce an unbearable anxiety particularly if it upsets the applecart, and if a desirable outcome is not readily available or rapidly achieved.

In spite of all the justifiable and not so justifiable resistance to change, design thinking, as its originators tell educators, is based on "the fundamental belief that we all can create change—no matter how big a problem, how little time or how small a budget."

This optimistic note emerges from the idea of design thinking as it favors small, easily manageable steps by a group of individuals who come together for a common cause, and try out something new without any fear of failure. They are going to learn from and build on their failure until they reach their desired goal. The kind of context-sensitive modular model that is being advocated here empowers local practitioners because they are the ones who bring to the task of model making much needed local knowledge and lived experience.

Instead of assuming that teachers and teacher educators are helpless onlookers who let others make decisions for them, it is instructive to recognize that they are constantly playing the role of change agents, whether they know it or not, whether they acknowledge it or not. They are relentlessly exercising their active agency as members of communities of practice, and communities of inquiry (see Chapter 5 for details). They are constantly engaged in projects of personal and professional transformation. As an in-depth study on teacher experience reveals, it

> is relatively common for teachers to talk about personal transformations having taken place in a dramatic fashion, using expressions such as, "It just happened overnight," or "The lights were suddenly switched on." Changes such as these can occur at any point in a teacher's career. One teacher talked about a personal transformation having occurred after she had been teaching for a few months, another after she had been teaching for several years, and a third after eight years.
>
> *(Senior 2006: 67)*

We have all along been engaged in a relentless pursuit of continuous quality improvement. Change is an integral part of that pursuit. As I have stated elsewhere:

> when we allow ourselves to be guided by bright distant stars, and not by dim street lights, and, when we resist the temptation to be lulled by what is easily manageable and what is easily measurable, and are willing to work with doubts and uncertainties, then, change becomes less onerous and more desirous.
>
> *(Kumaravadivelu 2006b: 226)*

7.4 Closings and Openings

As I write the last words of this book, I seek the reader's forbearance, because I wish to indulge in some contemplative thoughts. I began the first chapter of this book with a lead quotation from French philosopher Michel Serres who reminds us rather elegantly that "a cartload of bricks is not a house; we want a principle, a system, an integration" (2004: 2). What I have attempted to do in this book-length work is to collect some bricks scattered all over the professional literatures in several related fields, and use them to build a house. In laying the foundation with governing principles (particularity, practicality, and possibility), in cementing the structure with global perspectives (postnational, postmodern, postcolonial, post-transmission, and postmethod), and in constructing the entire edifice with interconnected modules (knowing, analyzing, recognizing, seeing, and doing), I am guided by the philosophical meditations of John Dewey and Paulo Friere, by the poststructural theories of Michel Foucault and Pierre Bourdieu, and by the postcolonial critiques of Edward Said and Gayatri Spivak. Pedagogical insights of numerous scholars in the fields of education and TESOL constituted an immense support system.

In many ways, the essentials of the modular model I have presented in this book is no more than a work in progress. Therefore, there cannot be closings in the traditional sense of the term; there can only be openings. It is my fervent hope that this book will open up new pathways to progress, prompting teachers

> to push boundaries of theory and research – to seek out new paradigms, models and ways of framing education – while at the same time keeping an eye squarely on that which matters: teaching and learning in classrooms.
>
> *(Luke 2006: 2)*

I believe it is the responsibility of teacher educators to push the boundaries to create the conditions necessary for teachers to know, to analyze, to recognize, to do, and to see learning and teaching from a broader and deeper perspective. I also believe that the essentials of a model such as the one presented here will help student teachers become strategic thinkers as well as strategic practitioners. It will help them develop a holistic understanding of what happens in their classroom, so that, eventually, they will be able to construct their own theory of practice. This model combines the personal, the professional, the political, and the pedagogical because they are all interconnected. To help teachers see "the pattern that connects" is the primary task of teacher education. For teacher educators, carrying out this task is not just an option; it is indeed an obligation.

As part of my professional obligation, I believe I have tried to consistently act on the critical pedagogic assumption that "liberating education consists of acts of cognition, not transferrals of information" (Freire 1972: 60). My acts of cognition—my scholarly explorations—have been motivated by a desire to go beyond the comfort zones afforded by traditional thinking. It is this motivation that has been reflected in my work on postmethod pedagogy that seeks to direct practicing and prospective language teachers away from pedagogic dependence and towards pedagogic independence (Kumaravadivelu 2003b, 2006b). It is this motivation, reflected in my work on cultural realism that seeks to move the teaching of culture away from the superficialities of food, fashion, and festivals, and towards global cultural consciousness that is responsive to the political, religious, and cultural tensions stemming from the processes of cultural globalization (Kumaravadivelu 2008). It is this motivation that, I believe, is reflected in my current work on the essentials of a modular model that seeks to push language teacher education away from the perils of discrete, product-based, transmission-oriented approaches and towards the promise of holistic, process-based, transformation-oriented models.

I have all along believed that we should direct our acts of cognition towards confidently searching for what is desirable rather than comfortably settling for what is doable. All true innovations whether in art or science or technology start with the desirable, and then move towards finding ways and means of converting them into the doable, into the workable. If we gaze only at the doable, we may not get to the desirable, but it is the reverse orbit of going from the desirable to the doable that results in true knowledge production, in true human progress. The problematic path of innovation in education is no different.

I have also all along believed that change, positive change, arising out of desirable acts of cognition is not only possible, but is also inevitable. History tells us that change *will* come—"in the ripeness of time." With that encouraging thought, and in the spirit of the oft-quoted poetic musings from Omar Khayyam, I move on:

The Moving Finger writes; and having writ,
Moves on: nor all your Piety nor Wit
Shall lure it back to cancel half a line,
Nor all your Tears wash out a Word of it.

REFERENCES

Allwright, D. (1981). What do we want teaching materials for? *ELT Journal*, 36 (1), 5–19.

——(1986). Making sense of instruction: What's the problem? *Papers in Applied Linguistics-Michigan* 1, 1–10.

——(1991). The death of the method. *Working Paper # 10*. The Exploratory Practice Centre, The University of Lancaster, UK.

——(2003). Exploratory practice: rethinking practitioner research in language teaching. *Language Teaching Research*, 7, 113–41.

——(2005). From teaching points to learning opportunities and beyond. *TESOL Quarterly*, 39 (1), 9–31.

Argyris, C. (1992). *On Organizational Learning*. Cambridge, MA: Blackwell Publishers.

Aronowitz, S. (2009). Foreword. In S.L. Macrine (ed.) *Critical Pedagogy in Uncertain Times* (pp. ix–xi). London: Palgrave/Macmillan.

Atay, D. (2004). Collaborative dialogue with student teachers as a follow-up to teacher in-service education and training. *Language Teaching Research*, 2, 143–63.

Atay, D. & Ece, A. (2009). Multiple identities as reflected in English language education: The Turkish perspective. *Journal of Language, Identity, and Education*, 8, 21–34.

Au, S.Y. (1988). A critical appraisal of Gardner's social-psychological theory of second language (L2) learning. *Language Learning*, 38, 75–100.

Auerbach, E. (1992). *Making Meaning, Making Change: Participatory Curriculum Development for Adult ESL Literacy*. McHenry, IL: Delta Systems, Inc.

Bakhtin, M. (1981). *The Dialogic Imagination* (Trans. C. Emerson and M. Holquist). Austin: University of Texas Press.

Barkhuizen, G. (1998). Discovering learners' perceptions of ESL classroom teaching/ learning activities in a South African context. *TESOL Quarterly*, 32 (1), 85–108.

——(2009). Topics, aims, and constraints in English teacher research: A Chinese case study. *TESOL Quarterly*, 43 (1), 113–25.

Barkhuizen, G. & Wette, R. (2008). Narrative frames for investigating the experiences of language teachers. *System*, 36, 372–87.

Bartels, N. (2005). *Applied Linguistics and Language Teacher Education*. New York: Springer.

——(2006). *The Construct of Cognition in Second Language Teacher Education and Development*. Giessen: Giessener Elektronische Bibliothek.

Bartolome, L.I. (1994). Beyond the methods fetish: Toward a humanizing pedagogy. *Harvard Educational Review*, 64, 173–94.

Basturkmen, H., Loewen, S., & Ellis, R. (2004). Teachers' stated beliefs about incidental focus on form and their classroom practices. *Applied Linguistics*, 25 (2), 243–72.

Benesch, S. (2001). *Critical English for Academic Purposes: Theory, Politics, and Practice*. New Jersey: Lawrence Erlbaum.

Benson, P. (1997). The philosophy and politics of learner autonomy. In P. Benson and P. Voller (eds.) *Autonomy and Independence in Language Learning*. (pp. 18–34). London: Longman.

——(2006). Autonomy in language teaching and learning. *Language Teaching*, 40, 21–40.

Bereiter, C., & Scardamalia, M. (1993). *Surpassing Ourselves – An Inquiry into the Nature and Implications of Expertise*. Illinois: Open Court.

Bialystok, E. (2002). Cognitive processes of L2 users. In V.J. Cook (ed.) *Portraits of the L2 User*. (pp. 145–65). Clevedon: Multilingual Matters.

Block, D. (1994). A day in the life of class: Teachers/learner perceptions of task purpose in conflict. *System*, 22 (4), 473–86.

——(2000). Problematizing interview data: Voices in the mind's machine. *TESOL Quarterly*, 34 (4), 757–63.

Borg, M. (2001). Teacher belief. *ELT Journal*, 55 (2), 186–88.

Borg, S. (2006). *Teacher Cognition and Language Education*. London: Continuum.

——(2007). Research engagement in English language teaching. *Teaching and Teacher Education*, 23 (5), 731–47.

——(2009). English language teachers' conceptions of research. *Applied Linguistics*, 30 (3), 355–88.

Bourdieu, P., Passeron, J., & Martin, M. (1994). *Academic Discourse: Linguistic Misunderstanding and Professional Power*. Cambridge: Polity Press.

Boyles, D.R. (2006). Dewey's epistemology: An argument for warranted assertions, knowing, and meaningful classroom practice. *Educational Theory*, 56 (1), 57–68.

Brandt, C. (2007). Allowing for practice: A critical issue in TESOL teacher preparation. *ELT Journal*, 60 (4), 355–64.

Breen, M.P. (1991). Understanding the language teacher. In R. Phillipson, E. Kellerman, L. Selinker, M. Sharwood Smith & M. Swain (eds.) *Foreign/Second Language Pedagogy Research*. (pp. 213–33). Clevedon, UK: Multilingual Matters.

——(2001). Overt participation and covert acquisition in the language classroom. In M.P. Breen (ed.) *Learner Contributions to Language Learning*. (pp. 112–40). New York: Pearson Education.

Breen, M.P., Hird, B., Milton, M., Oliver, R., & Thwaite, A. (2001). Making sense of language teaching: Teachers' principles and classroom practices. *Applied Linguistics*, 22 (4), 470–501.

Brindley, G. (1984). *Needs Analysis and Objective Setting in the Adult Migrant Education Program*. Sydney: Adult Migrant Education Service.

Brumfit, C. (2001). *Individual Freedom in Language Teaching*. Oxford: Oxford University Press.

Butler, J. (1990). *Gender Trouble: Feminism and the Subversion of Identity*. New York: Routledge.

Canagarajah, S. (1999). *Resisting Linguistic Imperialism in English Teaching*. Oxford: Oxford University Press.

Chihara, T. & Oller, J.W. (1978). Attitudes and attained proficiency in EFL: A sociolinguistic study of adult Japanese speakers. *Language Learning*, 28, 55–68.

Chirkov, V. (2009). A cross-cultural analysis of autonomy in education: A self-determination theory perspective. *Theory and Research in Education*, 7 (2), 253–62.

Cilliers, P. (1998). *Complexity & Postmodernism*. London: Routledge.

Clandinin, D.J. (1992). Narrative and story in teacher education. In T. Russell & H. Munby (eds.) *Teachers and Teaching: From Classroom to Reflection*. (pp. 124–37). London: Falmer Press.

Clandinin, D.J. & Connelly, F.M. (1987). *Narrative Experience and the Study of Curriculum*. Washington, DC: The American Association of Colleges for Teacher Education.
——(2000). *Narrative Inquiry: Experience and Story in Qualitative Research*. San Francisco: Jossey-Bass.
Clarke, M.A. (2003). *A Place to Stand: Essays for Educators in Troubled Times*. Ann Arbor: University of Michigan Press.
——(2007). *Common Ground, Contested Territory: English Language Teaching in Troubled Times*. Ann Arbor: University of Michigan Press.
Cochran-Smith, M. and Zeichner, K.M. (eds.). (2005). *Studying Teacher Education*. Washington, DC: American Educational Research Association, and Mahwah, NJ: Lawrence Erlbaum.
Coetzee-Van Rooy, S. (2006). Integrativeness: Untenable for world Englishes learners. *World Englishes*, 25, 437–50.
Coleman, H. (1996). Autonomy and ideology in the English language classroom. In H. Coleman (ed.) *Society and the Language Classroom*. (pp. 1–15). Cambridge: Cambridge University Press.
Colnerud, G. (2006). Teacher ethics as a research problem: Syntheses achieved and new issues. *Teachers and Teaching: Theory and Practice*, 12 (3), 365–85.
Connelly, F.M. & Clandinin, D.J. (1990). Stories of experience and narrative inquiry. *Educational Researcher*, 19 (2), 1–14.
Corder, S.P. (1967). The significance of learners' errors. *International Review of Applied Linguistics*, 5, 161–70.
Cosh, J. (1999). Peer observation: A reflective model. *ELT Journal*, 53 (1), 22–27.
Crabbe, D. (2003). The quality of language learning opportunities. *TESOL Quarterly*, 37 (1), 9–34.
Crandall, J. (2000). Language teacher education. *Annual Review of Applied Linguistics*, 20, 34–55.
Crookes, G. (2003). *A Practicum in TESOL*. Cambridge: Cambridge University Press.
——(2009). *Values, Philosophies, and Beliefs in TESOL*. Cambridge: Cambridge University Press.
Crookes, G. & Chandler, P. (1999). *Introducing Action Research into Post-secondary Foreign Language Teacher Education* (NFLRC NetWork #10) Honolulu: University of Hawai'i, Second Language Teaching & Curriculum Center.
Crystal, D. (1997). *English as a Global Language*. Cambridge: Cambridge University Press.
Dam, L. (2007). Teacher education for learner autonomy. *Independence* 42, IATEFL Learner Autonomy SIG.
De Lissovoy, N. (2009). Toward a critical pedagogy of the global. In S.L. Macrine (ed.) *Critical Pedagogy in Uncertain Times*. (pp. 189–205). London: Palgrave/Macmillan.
Deci, E.L. & Ryan, R.M. (1985). *Intrinsic Motivation and Self-determination in Human Behavior*. New York: Plenum.
——(2000). The "what" and "why" of goal pursuits: Human needs and the self-determination of behavior. *Psychological Inquiry*, 11 (4), 227–68.
——(2008). Self determination theory overview. Retrieved Sept. 18, 2008 from http://www.ling.lancs.ac.uk/groups/crile/usefullinks.html
Design Thinking for Educators. (2011). www.ideo.com.
Dewey, J. (1916). Introduction to *Essays in Experimental Logic*. In J. Boydstone (ed.) *The Middle Works (1899–1924)*. Carbondale: Southern Illinois University Press.
Dewey, J. (1922). *Human Nature and Conduct*. New York: Henry Holt & Co.
——(1933). *How We Think*. Boston: D.C. Heath.
Dewey, J. & Bentley, A. (1949). *Knowing and the Known*. Boston: Beacon Press.
Diamond, C.T.P. (1993). In-service education as something more: A personal construct approach. In P. Kahaney, L. Perry and J. Janangelo (eds.) *Theoretical and Critical Perspectives on Teacher Change*. (pp. 45–66). Norwood: Ablex.

Dörnyei, Z. (2009). The L2 motivational system. In Z. Dörnyei & E. Ushioda (eds.) *Motivation, Language Identity and the L2 Self.* (pp. 9–42). Bristol: Multilingual Matters.

Dörnyei, Z., & Ushioda, E. (eds.) (2009). *Motivation, Language Identity and the L2 Self.* Bristol: Multilingual Matters.

Doyle, W. (1986). Classroom management. In M.C. Wittrock (ed.) *Handbook of Research on Teaching.* (3rd ed.; pp. 392–431). New York: Macmillan.

——(1997). Heard any really good stories lately? A critique of the critics of narrative in educational research. *Teaching and Teacher Education,* 13 (1), 93–99.

——(2006). Ecological approaches to classroom management. In C.M Evertson & C.S. Weinstein (eds.) *Handbook of Classroom Management: Research, Practice, and Contemporary Issues.* (pp. 97–125). Mahwah, NJ: Lawrence Erlbaum.

Edge, J. (ed.) (2001). *Action Research.* Washington, DC: TESOL.

——(2002). *Continuing Cooperative Development.* Ann Arbor: University of Michigan Press.

——(2003). Imperial troopers and servants of the lord: A vision of TESOL for the 21st century. *TESOL Quarterly,* 37 (4), 701–9.

——(2011). *The Reflexive Teacher Educator in TESOL.* New York: Routledge.

Elbaz, F. (1983). *Teacher Thinking: A Study of Practical Knowledge.* London: Croom Helm.

Elliott, A. (2009). Series editor's foreword. In H. Ferguson, *Self-Identity and Everyday Life.* (pp. vii–x). New York: Routledge.

Elliott, J. (1991). *Action Research for Educational Change.* Buckingham: Open University Press.

——(1993). *Reconstructing Teacher Education: Teacher Development.* London: Falmer.

Ellis, R. (1992). *Second Language Acquisition and Language Pedagogy.* Clevedon: Multilingual Matters.

——(2001). The metaphorical constructions of second language learners. In M.P. Breen (ed.) *Learner Contributions to Language Learning.* (pp. 65–85). New York: Pearson Education.

——(2006). Current issues in the teaching of grammar: An SLA perspective. *TESOL Quarterly,* 40, 83–107.

——(2010). Second language acquisition, teacher education and language pedagogy. *Language Teaching,* 43 (2), 182–201.

Emerson, R.W. (1903). *Essays.* Volumes 1–2. Boston: Houghton, Mifflin and Company.

Evertson, C.M. & Weinstein, C.S. (2006). Classroom management as a field of inquiry. In C.M. Evertson & Weinstein C. S. (eds.) *Handbook of Classroom Management: Research, Practice, and Contemporary Issues.* (pp. 3–15). Mahwah, NJ: Lawrence Erlbaum.

——(eds.) (2006). *Handbook of Classroom Management: Research, Practice, and Contemporary Issues.* Mahwah, NJ: Lawrence Erlbaum.

Exploratory Practice (n.d.) *Exploratory Practice website.* www.ling.lancs.ac.uk/groups/cirile/EPCentre.

Fairclough, N. (1992). *Critical Language Awareness.* London: Longman.

——(1995). *Critical Discourse Analysis: The Critical Study of Language.* London: Longman.

Fanselow, J. (1977). Beyond "Rashomon" – conceptualizing and describing the teaching act. *TESOL Quarterly,* 11 (1), 17–39.

——(1990). "Let's see": Contrasting conversations about teaching. In J.C. Richards & D. Nunan (eds.) *Second Language Teacher Education.* New York: Cambridge University Press.

Farrell, T.S.C. (2007). Failing the practicum: Narrowing the gap between expectations and reality with reflective practice. *TESOL Quarterly,* 41 (1), 193–201.

——(2008). Here's the book, go teach the class': ELT practicum support. *RELC Journal,* 39, 226–41.

——(2011). Exploring the professional role identities of experienced ESL teachers through reflective practice. *System,* 39, 54–62.

Farrell, T.S.C. & Lim, P.C. (2005). Conceptions of grammar teaching: A case study of teachers' beliefs and classroom practices. *TESL-EJ,* 9 (2), 1–12.

Fenstermacher, G.D. (1979). A philosophical consideration of recent research on teacher effectiveness. *Review of Research in Education,* 6, 157–85.

——(1994). The knower and the known: The nature of knowledge in research on teaching. *Review of Research in Education*, 20, 3–56.

Ferguson, H. (2009). *Self-Identity and Everyday Life*. London: Routledge.

Fischman, G.E. (2009). Forword. In S.L. Macrine (ed.) *Critical Pedagogy in Uncertain Times*. (pp. 207–15). London: Palgrave/Macmillan.

Foucault, M. (1972). *The Archaelogy of Knowledge and the Discourse on Language*. (A.M. Sheridan Smith, Trans.). New York: Pantheon Books.

——(1980). *Power/Knowledge: Selected Interviews and Other Writings, 1972–77*. New York: Pantheon.

Freeman, D. (1998). *Doing Teacher Research*. New York: Heinle & Heinle.

Freire, P. (1972). *Pedagogy of the Oppressed*. London: Penguin.

——(1989). *Education for the Critical Conscious*. New York: Continuum.

Gardner, R.C. (1985). *Social Psychological and Second Language Learning: The Role of Attitudes and Motivation*. London: Edward Arnold.

Gardner, R.C. & Lambert, W.E. (1972). *Attitudes and Motivation in Second Language Learning*. Rowley, MA: Newbury House.

Gardner, R.C. & MacIntyre, P.D. (1991). An instrumental motivation in language study: Who says it isn't effective? *Studies in Second Language Acquisition*, 13, 57–72.

Gardner, R.C., Day, J.B., & MacIntyre, P.D. (1992). Integrative motivation, induced anxiety, and language learning in a controlled environment. *Studies in Second Language Acquisition*, 14, 197–214.

Garton, S. (2008). Teacher beliefs and interaction in the language classroom. In S. Garton, & K. Richards (eds.) *Professional Encounters in TESOL*. (pp. 67–86). London: Palgrave Macmillan.

Gee, J. (1994). Orality and literacy: From the savage mind to ways with words. In J. Maybin (ed.) *Language and Literacy in Social Practice*. Clevedon, UK: The Open University.

Geertz, C. (1973). *The Interpretation of Cultures*. New York: Basic Books.

——(1983). *Local Knowledge: Further Essays in Interpretive Anthropology*. New-York: Basic Books.

Giroux, H.A. (1988). *Teachers as Intellectuals: Toward a Critical Pedagogy of Learning*. Boston: Bergin & Harvey.

Graddol, D. (2006). *English Next*. London: The British Council.

Griffiths, C. (ed.) (2008). *Lessons from Good Language Learners*. Cambridge University Press.

Halliday, M.A.K. (1973). *Explorations in the Functions of Language*. London: Arnold.

Hansen, D.T. (2001). *Exploring the Moral Heart of Teaching*. New York: Teachers College Press.

——(2004). A poetics of teaching. *Educational Theory*, 54 (2), 119–42.

Hardt, M., & Negri, A. (2000). *Empire*. Cambridge, MA: Harvard University Press.

Hardy, B. (1968). Toward a poetics of fiction. *Novel*, 2, 5–14.

Hargreaves, A. (1994). *Changing Teachers, Changing Times*. New York: Teachers College Press.

Hedgcock, J. (2002). Toward a socioliterate approach to language teacher education. *Modern Language Journal*, 86, 299–317.

Held, V. (2006). *The Ethics of Care: Personal, Political, Global*. Oxford: Oxford University Press.

Hobsbawm, E. (2007). *Globalisation, Democracy and Terrorism*. London: Abacus.

Holec, H. (1981). *Autonomy and Foreign Language Learning*. Oxford: Pergamon.

——(1988). *Autonomy and Self-Directed Learning: Present Fields of Application*. Strasbourg, Council of Europe.

Human Development Report. (1999). Globalization with a human face. NY: United Nations Development Programme & Oxford University Press.

Hutchinson, T. & Waters, A. (1987). *English for Specific Purposes*. Cambridge: Cambridge University Press.

Ideo (2011). *Design Thinking for Educators*. Retrieved from www.ideo.com, June 23, 2011.

Ilieva, R. (2010). Non-native English-speaking teachers' negotiations of program discourses in their construction of professional identities within a TESOL program. *The Canadian Modern Language Review*, 66 (3), 343–69.

Jenkins, R. (1996). *Social Identity*. London: Routledge.

Johnson, K.E. (2006). The sociocultural turn and its challenges for second language teacher education. *TESOL Quarterly*, 40 (1), 235–57.

Johnson, K.E. & Golombek, P. (2002). *Teachers' Narrative Inquiry as Professional Development*. Cambridge: Cambridge University Press.

Johnston, B. (2003). *Values in English Language Teaching*. Mahwah, NJ: Lawrence Erlbaum.

Kachru, B.B. (1983). *The Indianization of English*. New Delhi: Oxford University Press.

Kincheloe, J.L. (1993). *Toward a Critical Politics of Teacher Thinking*. Westport: Bergin & Garvey.

——(2009). Contextualizing the madness: A critical analysis of the assault on teacher education and schools. In S.L. Groenke &. J.A. Hatch (eds.) *Critical Pedagogy and Teacher Education in the Neoliberal Era*. (pp. 19–36). New York: Springer.

Kontopoulos, K. (1993). *The Logics of Social Structures*. Cambridge: Cambridge University Press.

Krishnaswamy, N. & Burde, A. (1998). *The Politics of Indians' English: Linguistic Colonialism and the Expanding English Empire*. Delhi: Oxford University Press.

Kubota, R. & Lin, A. (eds.) (2009). *Race, Culture, and Identities in Second Language Education*. New York: Routledge.

Kumaravadivelu, B. (1991). Language learning tasks: teacher intention and learner interpretation. *ELT Journal*, 45 (2), 98–107.

——(1994). The postmethod condition: (E)merging strategies for second/foreign language teaching. *TESOL Quarterly*, 28, 27–48.

——(1999a). Critical classroom discourse analysis. *TESOL Quarterly*, 33, 453–84.

——(1999b). Theorising practice, practising theory: The role of critical classroom observation. In H. Trappes-Lomax and I. McGrath (eds.) *Theory in Language Teacher Education*. (pp. 33–45). London: Longman.

——(2001). Toward a postmethod pedagogy. *TESOL Quarterly*, 35, 537–60.

——(2002). From coloniality to globality: (Re)visioning English language education in India. *Indian Journal of Applied Linguistics*, 28 (2), 45–61.

——(2003a). A postmethod perspective on English language teaching. *World Englishes*, 22, 539–50.

——(2003b). *Beyond Methods: Macrostrategies for Language Teaching*. New Haven, CT: Yale University Press.

——(2006a). Dangerous liaison: Globalization, empire and TESOL. In J. Edge (ed.) *(Re) Locating TESOL in an Age of Empire*. (pp. 1–26). London: Palgrave/Macmillan.

——(2006b). *Understanding Language Teaching: From Method to Postmethod*. Mahwah, NJ: Lawrence Erlbaum.

——(2006c). TESOL methods: Changing tracks, challenging trends. *TESOL Quarterly*, 40 (1), 59–81.

——(2008). *Cultural Globalization and Language Education*. New Haven, CT: Yale University Press.

Kuo, I. (2011). Student perceptions of student interaction in a British EFL setting. *ELT Journal*, 65 (3), 281–90.

Kvernbekk, T. (2000). Seeing in practice: a conceptual analysis. *Scandinavian Journal of Educational Research*, 44 (4), 358–70.

Lamb, M. (2004). Integrative motivation in a globalizing world. *System*, 32, 3–19.

Larrivee, B. (2006). The convergence of reflective practice and effective classroom management. In C.M. Evertson & C. S. Weinstein (eds.) *Handbook of Classroom Management: Research, Practice, and Contemporary Issues*. (pp. 983–1001). Mahwah, NJ: Lawrence Erlbaum.

Lave, C.A. & March, J.G. (1993). *An Introduction to Models in the Social Sciences*. Lanham, MD: University Press of America.

Lave, J. (1988). *Cognition in Practice*. Cambridge: Cambridge University Press.

Lave, J. & Wenger, E. (1991). *Situated Learning: Legitimate Peripheral Participation*. Cambridge: Cambridge University Press.

Lee, I. (2009). Ten mismatches between teachers' beliefs and written feedback practice. *ELT Journal*, 63 (1), 13–22.

Lin, A. (ed.) (2008). *Problematizing Identity*. New York: Lawrence Erlbaum.

Lin, A. & Martin, P. (eds.) (2005). *Decolonisation, Globalisation: Language-in-Education Policy and Practice*. Clevedon: Multilingual Matters.

Little, D. (1991). *Learner Autonomy 1: Definitions, Issues and Problems*. Dublin: Authentik.

——(2009). Language learner autonomy and the European language portfolio: Two L2 English examples. *Language Teaching*, 42 (2), 222–33.

Littlewood, W. (1981). *Communicative Language Teaching: An Introduction*. Cambridge: Cambridge University Press.

——(1999). Defining and developing autonomy in East Asian contexts. *Applied Linguistics*, 20 (1), 71–94.

Lortie, D. (1975). *School Teacher*. Chicago: University of Chicago Press.

Luke, A. (2006). Why pedagogies? *Pedagogies: An International Journal*, 1, 1–5.

Lukmani, Y. (1972). Motivation to learn and language proficiency. *Language Learning*, 22, 261–73.

Lyons, Z. (2009). Imagined identity and the L2 Self in the French foreign legion. In Z. Dornyei & E. Ushioda (eds.) *Motivation, Language Identity and L2 Self*. (pp. 248–73). Bristol: Multilingual Matters.

Lyotard, J-F. (1989). *The Postmodern Condition: A Report on Knowledge*. Minneapolis: University of Minnesota Press.

Lytle, S.L. & Cochran-Smith, M. (1990). Learning from teacher research: A working typology. *Teachers College Record*, 92 (1), 83–103.

Macedo, D. (1994). Preface. In P. McLaren and C. Lankshear (eds.) *Conscientization and Resistance*. (pp. 1–8). New York: Routledge.

Mahboob, A. (2009). English as an Islamic language: A case study of Pakistani English. *World Englishes*, 28 (2), 175–89.

Marchenkova, L. (2005). Language, culture, and self: The Bakhtin-Vygotsky encounter. In J.K. Hall., G. Vitanova & L. Marchenkova (eds.) *Dialogue with Bakhtin on Second and Foreign Language Learning: New Perspectives*. (pp. 171–87). Mahwah, NJ: Lawrence Erlbaum.

Martin, J. (2007). The selves of educational psychology: Conceptions, contexts, and critical considerations. *Educational Psychologist*, 42 (2), 79–89.

McCrum, R. (2010). *Globish: How the English Language Became the World's Language*. London: W.W. Norton & Company.

McKay, S.L. (2006). *Researching Second Language Classrooms*. Mahwah, NJ: Lawrence Erlbaum.

McLaren, P. (1995a). Collisions with otherness: "Traveling" theory, postcolonial criticism, and the politics of ethnographic practice – The mission of the wounded ethnographer. In P. McLaren, & J. Giarelli (eds.) *Critical Theory and Educational Research*. (pp. 271–99). New York: State University of New York Press.

——(1995b). *Critical Pedagogy and Predatory Culture*. London: Routledge.

Morgan, B. (1998). *The ESL Classroom: Teaching, Critical Practice, and Community*. Toronto: Toronto University Press.

Murray, J. (2009). Teacher competencies in the postmethod landscape: The limits of competency-based training in TESOL teacher education. *Prospect*, 4 (1), 17–29.

Nakata, M. (2003). Some thoughts on literacy issues in indigenous contexts. *The Australian Journal of Indigenous Education*, 31, 7–15.

Nash, R.J. (2005). Foreword. In B. Zubay & J.F. Soltis, *Creating the Ethical School: A Book of Case Studies*. New York: Teachers College Press.

Nespor, J. (1987). The role of beliefs in the practice of teaching. *Journal of Curriculum Studies*, 19 (4), 317–28.

Niemiec, C. & Ryan, R.M. (2009). Autonomy, competence, and relatedness in the class-room. Applying self-determination theory to educational practice. *Theory and Research in Education*, 7 (2), 133–44.

Noddings, N. (1984). *Caring: A Feminine Approach to Ethics and Moral Education*. Berkeley, CA: University of California Press.

——(1999). Care, justice and equity. In M.S. Katz, N. Noddings & K.A. Strike (eds.) *Justice and Caring: The Search for Common Ground in Education*. (pp. 7–20). New York: Teachers College Press.

——(2010). Moral education in an age of globalization. *Educational Philosophy and Theory*, 42 (4), 390–96.

Norton, B. (2000). *Identity and Language Learning*. London: Longman.

Norton, B. & Toohey, K. (eds.) (2004). *Critical Pedagogies and Language Learning*. Cambridge: Cambridge University Press.

Nunan, D. (1989). *Designing Tasks for the Communicative Classroom*. Cambridge: Cambridge University Press.

O'Hanlon, C. (1993). The importance of an articulated personal theory of professional development. In J. Elliott (ed.) *Reconstructing Teacher Education: Teacher Development*. (pp. 243–355). London: The Falmer Press.

O'Malley, J.M. & Chamot, A.U. (1990). *Learning Strategies in Second Language Acquisition*. Cambridge: Cambridge University Press.

Orland-Barak, L. (2006). Convergent, divergent and parallel dialogues in mentors' professional conversations. *Teachers and Teaching: Theory and Practice*, 12 (1), 13–33.

Orland-Barak, L. & Leshem, S. (2009). Observation in learning to teach: Forms of "seeing." *Teacher Education Quarterly*, 36 (3), 21–37.

Oxford, R. (1990). *Language Learning Strategies: What Every Teacher Should Know*. New York: Newbury House/Harper and Row.

——(2011). Strategies for learning a second or foreign language. *Language Teaching*, 44 (2), 167–80.

Pajares, M.F. (1992). Teachers' beliefs and educational research: Cleaning up a messy construct. *Review of Educational Research*, 62, 307–32.

Palmer, P.J. (1998). *The Courage to Teach: Exploring the Inner Landscape of a Teacher's Life*. San Francisco: Jossey-Bass Publishers.

Pavlenko, A. (2003). "I never knew I was a bilingual": Re-imagining teacher identities in TESOL. *Journal of Language, Identity, and Education*, 2 (4), 251–68.

——(2007). Autobiographic narratives as data in applied linguistics. *Applied Linguistics*, 28 (2), 163–88.

Pennycook, A. (1989). The concept of method, interested knowledge, and the politics of language teaching. *TESOL Quarterly*, 23, 589–618.

——(1997). Cultural alternatives and autonomy. In P. Benson & P. Voller (eds.) *Autonomy and Independence in Language Learning*. (pp. 35–53). London: Longman.

——(1998). *English and the Discourses of Colonialism*. New York: Routledge.

——(2001). *Critical Applied Linguistics: A Critical Introduction*. Mahwah, NJ: Lawrence Erlbaum.

Phan, L.H. (2007). Australian-trained Vietnamese teachers of English: Culture and identity formation. *Language, Culture and Curriculum*, 20 (1), 20–35.

Phillipson, R. (1992). *Linguistic Imperialism*. Oxford: Oxford University Press.

——(2003). *English-only Europe? Challenging Language Policy*. London: Routledge.

Phipps, S. & Borg, S. (2009). Exploring tensions between teachers' grammar teaching beliefs and practices. *System*, 37, 380–90.

Pinker, S. (1994). *The Language Instinct: How the Mind Creates Language*. New York: HarperPerennial.

Polanyi, M. (1958). *Personal Knowledge*. Chicago, IL: The University of Chicago Press.

——(1966). *The Tacit Dimension*. New York: Doubleday.

Prabhu, N.S. (1990). There is no best method – why? *TESOL Quarterly*, 24, 161–76.

Pratt, M.L. (1992). *Imperial Eyes: Travel Writing and Transculturation*. London and New York: Routledge.

Ramani, E., Chacko T., Singh, S.J., & Glendinning, E.H. (1988). An ethnographic approach to syllabus design: A case study of the Indian Institute of Science, Bangalore. *ESP Journal*, 7 (2), 81–90.

Reckling, F. (2001). Interpreted modernity: Weber and Taylor on values and modernity. *European Journal of Social Theory*, 4 (2): 153–76.

Reeve, J.M. & Halusic, M. (2009). How K-12 teachers can put self-determination theory principles into practice. *Theory and Research in Education*, 7, 145–54.

Richards, J.C. (ed.) (1998). *Teaching in Action: Case Studies from Second Language Classrooms*. Alexandria, VA: TESOL Inc.

Richards, K. (2006). "Being the teacher": Identity and classroom conversation. *Applied Linguistics*, 27 (1), 51–77.

——(2009). Trends in qualitative research in language teaching since 2000. *Language Teaching*, 42 (2), 147–80.

Richterich, R. (1984). A European unit/credit system for modern language learning by adults. In J. A. van Ek and J. L. M. Trim (eds.) *Across the Threshold Level*. (pp. 5–23). London: Pergamon.

Samuelowicz, K., & Bain, J.D. (2001). Revisiting academics' beliefs about teaching and learning. *Higher Education*, 41, 299–325.

Schön, D.A. (1983). *The Reflective Practitioner: How Professionals Think in Action*. New York: Basic Books.

Sen, A. (2006). *Identity and Violence: The Illusion of Destiny*. New York: Allen Lake.

Senior, R.M. (2006). *The Experience of Language Teaching*. Cambridge: Cambridge University Press.

Serres, M. (2004). *The Parasite* (trans. Lawrence R, Schehr). Minneapolis: University of Minnesota Press.

Shohamy, E. (1998). Critical language testing and beyond. *Studies in Educational Evaluation*, 24, 331–45.

Shulman, L.S. (1986a). Those who understand: Knowledge growth in teaching. *Educational Researcher*, 15 (2), 4–14.

——(1986b). Paradigms and research programs in the study of teaching. In M. Wittrock (ed.) *Handbook of Research on Teaching* (3rd ed.). (pp. 3–36). New York: Macmillan Publishing.

——(1987). Knowledge and teaching: Foundations for the new reform. *Harvard Educational Review*, 57 (1), 1–22.

Slimani, A. (1989). The role of topicalization in classroom language learning. *System*, 17 (2), 223–34.

Spratt, M. (1999). How good are we at knowing what learners like? *System*, 27, 141–55.

Spring, J. (2007). *Pedagogies of Globalization: The Rise of the Educational Security State*. Mahwah, NJ: Lawrence Erlbaum.

Sri Aurobindo (1939/2001). *The Essential Aurobindo: Writings of Sri Aurobindo*. Edited by R.A. McDermott (2001). Canada: Lindisfarne Books.

Stevick, E.W. (1980). *Teaching Languages: A Way and Ways*. Rowley, MA: Newbury House.

Stewart, T. (2006). Teacher-researcher collaboration or teachers' research? *TESOL Quarterly*, 40, 421–30.

——(2007). Teachers and learners evaluating course tasks together. *ELT Journal*, 61 (3), 256–66.

Taylor, C. (1989). *Sources of the Self: The Making of the Modern Identity*. Cambridge: Cambridge University Press.

——(1994). Reply and re-articulation. In J. Tully (ed.) *Philosophy in the Age of Pluralism: The Philosophy of Charles Taylor in Question*. (pp. 213–57). Cambridge: Cambridge University Press.

TESOL Quarterly, 42, June 2008. Symposium on "theorizing TESOL."

Transforming Teacher Education: Redefined Professionals for 21st Century Schools. (2008). The International Alliance of Leading Education Institutes. Singapore: National Institute of Education.

Tsui, A.B.M. (2003). *Understanding Expertise in Teaching: Case Studies of ESL Teachers.* Cambridge: Cambridge University Press.

Ulichny, P. & Schoener, W. (1996). Teacher/researcher collaboration from two perspectives. *Harvard Educational Review*, 66 (3), 496–524.

Ushioda, E. (2006). Language motivation in a reconfigured Europe: Access, identity and autonomy. *Journal of Multilingual and Multicultural Development*, 27 (2), 148–61.

Ushioda, E. & Dörnyei, Z. (2009). Motivation, language identities and the L2 self: A theoretical overview. In Z. Dornyei & E. Ushioda (eds.) *Motivation, Language Identity and the L2 Self.* (pp. 1–9), Buffalo: Multilingual Matters.

van Manen, M. (1977). Linking ways of knowing with ways of being practical. *Curriculum Inquiry*, 6, 205–28.

——(1991). *The Tact of Teaching: The Meaning of Pedagogical Thoughtfulness.* Albany: State University of New York Press.

Varghese, M. (2001). Professional development as site for the conceptualization and negotiation of bilingual teacher identities. In B. Johnston and S. Irujo (eds.) *Research and Practice in Language Teacher Education.* (pp. 213–32). Minneapolis: University of Minnesota, Center for Advanced Research in Second Language Acquisiton.

Vygotsky, L.S. (1986). *Thought and Language.* Cambridge, MA: MIT Press.

Wajnryb, R. (1992). *Classroom Observation Tasks.* Cambridge: Cambridge University Press.

Wallace, M. (1998). *Action Research for Language Teachers.* Cambridge: Cambridge University Press.

Walsh, S. (2003). Developing interactional awareness in the second language classroom through teacher self-evaluation. *Language Awareness*, 12 (2), 124–42.

——(2006). *Investigating Classroom Discourse.* London: Routledge.

Weeden, C. (1997). *Feminist Practice and Poststructuralist Theory.* London: Blackwell.

Wells, G. (1999). *Dialogic Inquiry.* Cambridge: Cambridge University Press.

Wenger, E. (1998). *Communities of Practice: Learning, Meaning, and Identity.* Cambridge: Cambridge University Press.

Widdowson, H.G. (1990). *Aspects of Language Teaching.* Oxford: Oxford University Press.

Wong, R.M.H. (2009). Try to describe the main point of your lesson: Student perception and identification of learning objectives in English lessons. *Reflections on English Language Teaching*, 8 (2), 73–88.

Woods, D. (1996). *Teacher Cognition in Language Teaching.* Cambridge: Cambridge University Press.

Wright, T. (2005). *Classroom Management in Language Education.* London: Palgrave Macmillan.

——(2010). Second language teacher education: Review of recent research on practice. *Language Teaching*, 43 (3), 259–96.

Zeichner, K. (2005). Becoming a teacher educator: A personal perspective. *Teaching and Teacher Education*, 21, 117–24.

Zembylas, M. (2003). Emotions and teacher identity: A poststructural perspective. *Teachers and Teaching: Theory and Practice*, 9 (3), 213–38.

INDEX